The Apocaly
and The Assum

The Apocalypse of Baruch
and The Assumption of Moses

Original translations by
R.H. Charles
&
William John Ferrar

Introduced by
R.A. Gilbert

WEISERBOOKS
Boston, MA/York Beach, ME

This edition first published in 2006 by
Red Wheel/Weiser, LLC
York Beach, ME
With offices at:
368 Congress Street
Boston, MA 02210
www.redwheelweiser.com

Library of Congress Cataloging-in-Publication Data
available upon request.

ISBN 1-57863-363-X

Printed in Canada
TCP

13 12 11 10 09 08 07 06
 8 7 6 5 4 3 2 1

CONTENTS

Introduction

The biblical Baruch, the son of Neriah, who acted as a faithful scribe to the prophet Jeremiah, lived in the time of Nebuchadnezzar, the Babylonian king (605–562 B.C.) who destroyed the Temple and took the Israelites into captivity. But all of the books that bear his name were written more than six hundred years after his death. Why, then, did the real authors hide their names and assume the name of a man who was a minor figure among the ranks of the prophets and patriarchs?

To answer that question we must consider the nature of the books in question. The best known appears in the Apocrypha[1] as *The Book of Baruch*. This claims to be by Baruch the scribe of Jeremiah, but was almost certainly written by several authors and was composed towards the end of the first century A.D. It is made up of four distinct sections: a narrative introduction, setting out its alleged origin and its purpose; a confessional, penitential prayer; a hymn of praise to Wisdom, personified as the Torah; and a concluding psalm,

1 The Apocrypha (from the Greek, αποκρυφα, 'hidden' or 'concealed') comprises those books of the Bible that were accepted by the early Christian Church as forming part of the Greek version of the Old Testament (the Septuagint), but which were excluded from the Hebrew Bible. In the version of the Bible used in the Roman Catholic Church, the apocryphal books, described as 'deuterocanonical' (*i.e.* accepted as canonical books at a later date than those in the Jewish canon of scripture) form part of the Old Testament. Among Protestant Churches, which tend to use biblical translations from the Greek, these books sit, somewhat uneasily, as a separate section between the Old and New Testaments.

offering consolation and encouragement to the Jews in exile. Given the date of composition, it is effectively addressed to the Jewish community in Palestine, which was then in despair at the destruction of Jerusalem by Titus.

There are numerous other texts ascribed to Baruch, and for ease of reference *The Book of Baruch* is usually styled '1 Baruch'. Of these other texts some are known only by references and occasional quotation in patristic works. The most interesting of these — if it could be recovered — would unquestionably be the gnostic book *Baruch*, described very briefly by Hippolytus in his *Philosophumena,* or *The Refutation of All Heresies.*[2] This book is by the gnostic Justinus, a leader of the Ophites, and Baruch is described as the third angel of God. Not only does he command Adam and Eve not to eat the fruit of the Tree of the Knowledge of Good and Evil, but he is also sent by Elohim to teach Jesus what to preach and to warn him of the wickedness of Naas, the Serpent. The only connection with other Baruch literature is the name.

Quite different from this is a Latin text referred to by Cyprian[3] in his *Testimonia*. He gives a short but significant quotation from a lost work that was clearly based on the most important of the Baruch texts, the *Apocalypse of Baruch*, which exists in not one but three forms. Before we examine these different versions, however, it is necessary to determine what constitutes an Apocalypse, and to consider the nature and meaning of apocalyptic literature.

2 This was originally attributed to Origen but is now accepted as being the work of Hippolytus, c. A.D. 220. An English translation, by F. Legge, was published in 1921.

3 St. Cyprian was a major figure in the field of early Christian literature. He became Bishop of Carthage in 248 A.D. and in the same year issued the pastoral work, *Testimonia ad Quirinum*. He was martyred in A.D. 258.

The Greek word 'apocalypse' (σψμβολ) means a revelation, or unveiling, and a book prefixed by the title 'Apocalypse' thus claims to be an unveiling of future events — a revelation of what is to come as part of the divine plan. To this extent apocalyptic literature is a special development, or extension of prophetic texts. Both these forms of religious text agree in claiming divine inspiration, and a valid communication of the form and purpose of the Divine Will, the nature of the Kingdom of God, and God's law for man.

There are, however, significant differences. Biblical prophecy is conditional, and often short-term. Events in the unspecified but distant future, such as the coming of the Messiah, may be foretold, but the message of the prophet is usually that if the people do not follow the Will of God, and change their ways *now*, then dire consequences will follow, and follow quickly. Even so, it is an open future, and the prophet tends to be an optimist — for him, this material world is God's world, in which His goodness and truth will be manifested in due time.

But while the prophet is primarily concerned with the present and with this world, the apocalyptic writer looks to the far future — to the last days of this world — and to the next world: to the rewarding of the righteous and the punishing of the wicked at the end of time. There is an inevitability about an apocalypse: God's punishment upon the oppressors of his chosen people is already determined and it will be worked out in a manner and at a time of His choosing. What each apocalypse does is to set out an individual narrative of the process by which the Final Judgment comes about. The fate of nations is certain: the oppressors of Israel, or of the Church, will be condemned to eternal destruction. And as with nations so with individuals. Among the chosen people, those who are righteous, who have obeyed the Law throughout their time of suffering in this life, will be saved for eternal life with God.

Such determinism is a characteristic of apocalyptic texts, but there are differences in the theology of Jewish and Christian apocalypses. Christianity encompasses the Gentiles as well as the Israelites and salvation is possible to all, but not all Christians accepted (as some still do not) that everyone either could or would be saved. The pernicious doctrine of pre-destination — that from eternity God has foreordained every individual either to salvation or damnation — avoids the necessary destruction of nations, but gives no guarantee of salvation according to one's works. But for Christian and Jew alike the object of apocalypse was to resolve the paradox of the righteousness of God and the endless temporal suffering of His people on earth.

It was also imperative for the writer that the people of his own community should read and act upon what he wrote. To this end two things were necessary. The narrative should be powerful and immediate, and the text should be attributed to a figure of patristic or prophetic authority. The first was easily managed. Apocalyptic texts include revelations from God mediated by angelic beings, accounts of journeys in a supernatural world, and real or symbolic descriptions of future catastrophes and judgments on a cosmic scale. Nor is it necessary to ascribe the visions of the writer to his imagination alone; there is the possibility, even the probability, that he is recounting visionary experiences that he had personally undergone. Against this it may be argued that some apocalyptic texts have internal inconsistencies and contradictions that suggest a text woven into a whole from disparate parts created by a number of writers. But even if this was so, the individual visions may retain their own integrity; and the very nature of visionary experience is such that absolute consistency is unlikely to be maintained by any one person. And whatever stance one may choose to take, visions remain a central and essential part of apocalyptic texts.

For some texts the author is contemporary with them, as with the *Revelation of St. John the Divine*, in which all of the visionary, angelic, symbolic and supernatural elements are present. The Christian communities who read his words knew, trusted and respected him, and were thus disposed to take seriously what he had written. Matters were different for the Jews. During the period when the cycle of Roman oppression, revolt and further oppression seemed endless, the dispersed Jewish communities within the Roman Empire were in a state of despair and needed the support and comfort that apocalyptic writing could bring, but until Rabbinic Judaism had become well-established there were few, if any, contemporary figures of spiritual authority. And so the apocalypses were credited to patriarchs and prophets: to Adam, Enoch, and Abraham; to Elijah, Ezekiel and Ezra. And to Baruch.

Why Baruch? First, he was closely associated with Jeremiah, who was among the greatest of the prophets and who had correctly predicted the downfall of Babylon. Then, he was one of those who remained in ruined Jerusalem, so that a vision based upon the city of that time would fit well with his name. Further, he had called upon the Lord in his despair: 'Woe is me now! For the Lord hath added grief to my sorrow; I fainted in my sighing, and I find no rest.' (Jeremiah 45:3) — and the Lord had answered him with words of hope for the future. What better name for a vision of judgement upon the oppressor? Or rather, visions, for the texts are quite different.

The earliest version of the *Apocalypse of Baruch* is Greek [*3 Baruch*]. It was known from a reference in Origen, but was lost to sight until 1896 when the Rev. Cuthbert Butler identified a manuscript in the British Museum as the Greek *Baruch* and brought it to the notice of M.R. James, who edited the text and published it in 1897.[4] Although this short text (it runs to seventeen very short chapters) has been dated to the 2nd century A.D., the only known manuscripts are from the 15th and 16th centuries. There are also a number of Slavonic manuscripts from the 13th century onwards which are basically similar in content but with sufficient variation to indicate that they came from a different Greek text that is now lost.[5] Partly on textual grounds, and partly because the complex symbolism of the text lends itself to a variety of interpretations, it is still unclear as to whether *3 Baruch* should be treated as a Christian Apocalypse, a Jewish-gnostic work, or a Jewish text with minor Christian interpolations. What distinguishes *3 Baruch* from the Syriac version, from which the present English translation has been made, is the journey of Baruch through five heavens. This is absent from the Syriac text.

The revelations in the Greek version are mediated by the angel Phamiel (*i.e.* Phanuel, as in *1 Enoch*), who conducts Baruch through five heavens[6], explaining their mysteries as

4 M.R. James (Ed.), *Apocrypha Anecdota*. Second Series. Cambridge University Press, 1897 (Vol. V of *Texts and Studies Contributions to Biblical and Patristic Literature*. Edited by J. Armitage Robinson) pp 83–94. James's introduction to the text is on pp *li–lxxi*.

5 The Slavonic and Greek texts are given in parallel English translations in J.H. Charlesworth (Ed.), *The Old Testament Pseudepigrapha*. Volume 1 Apocalyptic Literature and Testaments. London, Darton, Longman & Todd, 1983, pp 662–679.

they go. The first two heavens contain the wicked who are being punished, while in the third heaven is Hades, as an inverted Garden of Eden, with strange symbolic creatures, plus a Phoenix with the sun and the moon. The fourth heaven is a gathering place for the souls of the righteous, but Baruch is denied entrance to the fifth heaven, and thus to the presence of God. Finally he returns to earth to tell his people what he has seen and learned.

The Syriac version of the *Apocalypse of Baruch* [*2 Baruch*] is considerably longer than the Greek text and of far greater significance. For R.H. Charles it was a 'beautiful Apocalypse,' of which he wrote:

> In this Apocalypse we have almost the last noble utterance of Judaism before it plunged into the dark and oppressive years that followed the destruction of Jerusalem. .... But when our book was written, that evil and barren era had not yet set in; breathing thought and burning word had still their home in Palestine, and the hand of the Jewish artist was still master of its ancient cunning. (*The Apocrypha and Pseudepigrapha of the Old Testament in English*. Oxford, 1913, Vol. 2, p 470)

F.C. Burkitt, in his *Jewish and Christian Apocalypses* (Oxford, 1914), considered that *Baruch* was of great interest because

---

6 Origen calls for seven heavens in his reference to Baruch, but James was convinced that his text was the one in question: 'And I think our book is clearly the one referred to: for, though a seventh heaven is never reached in the prophet's progress, the book is evidently incomplete as we have it, and the existence of further heavens is implied.' (*op. cit.*, p *li*).

of the light that it throws,

> ...upon the state of mind of the Jews after the
> Destruction of Jerusalem, those who braced them-
> selves to remain loyal to the religion of their fathers,
> even after the downfall of the system upon which
> it had seemed to be founded. (p 42)

What, then, of the text itself?

It is, like many pseudepigraphic[7] texts, a composite work. By far the greater part of *2 Baruch* is a true apocalypse, but the final chapters (78 to 87) comprise *The Letter of Baruch, the son of Neriah, which he wrote to the Nine and a Half Tribes*. Of the Letter there are many surviving Syriac manuscripts — thirty-six in all — but there is only one Syriac text of the complete manuscript. This dates from the 6th century A.D. and is preserved in the Ambrosian Library at Milan. A few later extracts, which had been used as readings within the Jacobite Church[8], survive and there is an earlier, fourth-century fragment of the text in Greek among the thousands of papyri found at Oxyrhynchus, in Egypt, in 1897. One later manu-script, a free translation into Arabic, has been discovered at St.

7 'Pseudepigrapha' (*lit.* 'writings with false superscription') is the name given to some sixty-five texts that form a class of pseudonymous Jewish and early Christian religious works written in the centuries immediately before and after the time of Christ. Their real compilers, almost always unknown, chose to ascribe their works to patriarchs or prophets in order to give them a greater weight of authority. They are, however, extra-biblical, because none of the pseudepigrapha is included in the Canon of the Old Testament.

8 'Jacobites' was the name given to the early Church of Syria, after Jacob Baradaeus (c. 500–578) who established it as a national body. They were Monophysites, believing that the Incarnate Christ was wholly divine and did not have a human nature.

Catherine's Monastery in Sinai.

From its title we know that *2 Baruch* is a translation from Greek, but the language and content of the work points unquestionably to a Hebrew original. It was probably written early in the second century, since it is clear from the text (32:2–4) that the destruction of the second Temple, in A.D. 70, had already taken place. As to the author, the tenor of the text suggests that he was a Pharisee, living in Palestine and well acquainted with the rabbinic literature of his time. There can be no certainty as to his identity, but it has been suggested that he was one of the circle around the famous Rabbi Akiba, possibly Rabbi Joshua ben Hananiah (c. A.D. 40–125).

What is certain is that *3 Baruch* is a wholly Jewish work, written for the consolation and exhortation of the anguished Jewish community living in Palestine after the Roman destruction of Jerusalem. The ground of the hope he brings them is observance of the Law, for this will bring about the restoration of the people, the downfall of their enemies and the ultimate glorification of those who "have been justified through their obedience to [God's] Law" (51:3).

The book describes past, present and future events, and it can be divided easily and naturally into seven sections[9]. The text begins with the Babylonian destruction of Jerusalem — here ascribed to the angels of God — after the holy things of the Temple have been removed by another angel. When the Israelites, with Jeremiah, are taken into captivity Baruch remains behind. Then God tells Baruch why the people have been punished and what will be the fate of the wicked. After this Baruch fasts, and in answer to his prayers he is told of the twelve times of tribulation and of the Messianic era that

9 They comprise, respectively, the following chapters: I: 1–12; II: 13–20; III: 21–34; IV: 35–46; V: 47–52; VI: 53–76; and VII: 77–87.

will follow. He warns the people of what is to come and urges them to observe the Law.

In the fourth section Baruch sits down in the ruins of the Temple and experiences his vision of a forest in a plain surrounded by mountains. This 'forest of wickedness' is overcome by a spring flowing from a vine, which enters into a dialogue with the one remaining cedar tree until that, too, is destroyed and the plain is filled with flowers. When Baruch awakes the vision is explained to him by God, and he tells the people of the impending judgment. Baruch then fasts and prays again, and learns the nature of the future state of both the righteous and the wicked.

Baruch then receives a further vision, of a cloud, surrounded by lightning, from which dark and bright waters alternately pour down upon the earth and give rise to twelve rivers. The vision is explained to Baruch by the angel Ramiel, 'who presides over genuine visions'. Baruch then thanks God, Who bids him to teach the people and after forty days to ascend a mountain from which he will see all of the earth, and then be taken up into heaven.

The final section contains Baruch's letter to the nine and a half tribes. There should clearly be a second letter to the two and a half tribes in Babylon, but the book ends without it. It is thus possible that *2 Baruch* is incomplete in the form we have it, but R.H. Charles has argued convincingly that the missing letter does survive as the final part of the Book of Baruch (chapters 3 and 4).[10] But however we view the text, it remains, above all else, a powerful and passionate expression of abiding and sustaining faith in the face of almost overwhelming adversity.

10 R.H. Charles, *The Apocalypse of Baruch translated from the Syriac*. London, 1896, pp *lxv–lxvii*.

The desire of its author to bring comfort to his people and to show them how and why they must remain obedient to the Law in their faith and in their lives, is present also in the other translated text printed here. *The Assumption of Moses*, now generally styled *The Testament of Moses*, belongs to a class of pseudepigrapha, closely related to apocalyptic, that is categorised as "Testaments." These texts contain moral exhortation and a narrative, usually cast in the form of dramatic, prophetic visions of the future, illustrating the sufferings and tribulations of the Israelites, the ultimate downfall of their oppressors and the coming of the Messianic kingdom. As with apocalyptic texts they are attributed to one or more of the patriarchs, and are usually presented as recounting the last wishes — the testament — of the supposed author.

Only one text of *The Assumption of Moses* is known: a Latin translation surviving in a single manuscript copy. As with the full text of *2 Baruch*, this is preserved in the Ambrosian Library at Milan. The manuscript, which dates from the sixth century (although the style indicates that this translation originated in the previous century), is far from complete. It must also be viewed as the translation of a translation, for it was undoubtedly originally written in Hebrew — probably in the first century A.D.—from which it was translated first into Greek and then from the Greek into Latin.

Charles argued that the author was a "Pharisaic quietist," but later commentators have suggested an Essene source. Against this it should be noted that no fragments of the text have been found at Qumran, and the safest position on authorship is probably that of Priest, who thought it preferable 'to state simply that [the text] reflects the general outlook of the

11 J. Priest, 'Testament of Moses (First Century A.D.) A New Translation and Introduction', in J.H. Charlesworth (Ed.), *op. cit.* Vol. 1, p 922.

later Hasidic movement with a stress on apocalyptic motifs'[11].

The Assumption of Moses is presented as a farewell speech to Joshua, whom he has appointed as his successor. The future tribulations are set out in dramatic form throughout the twelve chapters, with far more historical allusions than are present in *2 Baruch*, and with the protagonists easily identified. Thus 'a king from the east' (3:1), is Nebuchadnezzar; 'one of those set over them' (4:1) is Daniel; 'kings ... called priests' (6:1) are the Hasmoneans; and 'a powerful king of the west' (6:8) is Varus, the governor of Syria.

Further on in Moses's narrative (chapter 9) comes the story of Taxo[12], a righteous man who prefers to die in the wilderness with his sons than to transgress the Law. Then the Lord's kingdom appears, the Devil is cast down, the angel (who is Michael) punishes the enemies of the righteous, and the earth is destroyed by the Lord while the people of Israel ascend to heaven. Here the narrative ends and Joshua laments that Moses is about to die, that no sepulchre can be fit for him, and that he — Joshua — is unfit to lead the Israelites. But Moses reminds him of God's providence and .... Here the text breaks off and we can only guess at its conclusion.

A suggested structure of the missing portion was proposed by R.H. Charles, who examined and collated all of the Greek fragments of the Assumption, and set out the following probable course of action:

1. [The archangel] Michael was commissioned to bury Moses.

2. Satan opposed the burial on the ground

(a) that he was the lord of matter and that

12 This is a corruption in the Latin text of 'Taxoc', a Greek form, by the substitution of letters, of Eleazar, for whom see the second Book of Maccabees.

accordingly the body should be rightfully handed over to him;

(b) that Moses was a murderer, having slain the Egyptian.

3. Michael having rebutted Satan's accusations proceeded to charge Satan with having instigated the serpent to tempt Eve.

4. Finally, all opposition having been overcome, the assumption took place in the presence of Joshua and Caleb, and in a very peculiar way. A two-fold presentation of Moses appeared: one was Moses in company with angels, the other was the dead body of Moses, being buried in the recesses of the mountains.[13]

This scenario neatly rounds off the narrative and emphasises the heavenly reward of the righteous.

But does all of this have a value for the reader of today? On several counts it certainly does. First, these texts are fascinating in their own right as works of creative literature, presenting a scintillating array of the hopes, fears and speculations of the people among whom they arose. Also, they are representative of the religious culture of their authors, and of the era in which Judaism was fashioned in its historic form and in which Christianity was born and came of age. As we are all, in one way or another, children of the Judaeo-Christian culture of the West, we deserve to have access to all aspects of the literature that is our heritage. It is also helpful to have

13 R.H. Charles, *Apocrypha and Pseudepigrapha of the Old Testament in English*. Oxford, 1913, Vol. 2, p 409.

this literature presented to us in plain and unadorned form, as few of us have the ability or inclination to benefit from a full critical apparatus to support the texts — or the means to pay for such expensive publications.

If we have a deeper interest in the spiritual message and implications of these texts, then a familiarity with them in their existing form is essential if we are to make sense of the new and unpredictable light that will be cast upon them as new imaging techniques enable ancient manuscripts to be read more fully and more accurately than was possible in the past. We must also remember that western spirituality — indeed, all spirituality — is grounded in the past, and that our experience of it is enriched when that past is opened up to us.

—R.A. Gilbert
Bristol, England, 2005

Bibliography

Burkitt, F.C. *Jewish and Christian Apocalypses* (The
    Schweich Lectures 1913) London, Oxford University
    Press, 1914

Charles, R.H. (Ed.) *Apocrypha and Pseudepigrapha of the
    Old Testament in English.* Oxford University Press,
    1913 2 volumes.

————. *The Apocalypse of Baruch, translated from the
    Syriac.* London, O.U.P., 1896

Charlesworth, J.H. (Ed.), *The Old Testament
    Pseudepigrapha.* London, Darton, Longman & Todd,
    1983 2 volumes.

James, M.R.(Ed.), *Apocrypha Anecdota.* Second Series.
    Cambridge University Press, 1897 (Vol. V of *Texts
    and Studies Contributions to Biblical and Patristic
    Literature.* Edited by J. Armitage Robinson)

————. *The Lost Apocrypha of the Old Testament.* London,
    Society for Promoting Christian Knowledge, 1920

Sparks, H.F.D. (Ed.), *The Apocryphal Old Testament.*
    Oxford, Clarendon Press, 1985

The Apocalypse of Baruch
Translated by R.H. Charles

Thick type indicates an emendation of the text.

[   ] = passages or words not from the hand of the original writer of the book.

(   ) = something supplied for the sake of clearness, but not belonging to the text.

⟨   ⟩ = a restoration of the text.

THE APOCALYPSE OF
BARUCH

[Translated from the Greek into Syriac.]

I. 1–IV. 1. Announcement of the coming Destruction of Jerusalem to Baruch.

I. And it came to pass in the twenty-fifth year of Jeconiah king of Judah, that the word of the Lord came to Baruch the son of Neriah, and said to him : 2. "Hast thou seen all that this people are doing to Me, that the evils which these two tribes which remained have done are greater than (those of) the ten tribes which were carried away captive ? 3. For the former tribes were forced by their kings to commit sin, but these two of themselves have been forcing and compelling their kings to commit sin. 4. For this reason, behold I bring evil upon this city, and upon its inhabitants, and it shall be removed from before Me for a time, and I will scatter this people among the Gentiles that they may do good to the Gentiles. 5. And My people shall be chastened, and the time will come when they will seek for the prosperity of their times.

II. "For I have said these things to thee that thou mayest bid Jeremiah, and all those who are like you, to retire from this city. 2. For your works are to this city as a firm pillar, and your prayers as a strong wall."

III. And I said : " O Lord, my Lord, have I come into the world for this purpose that I might see the evils of my mother ? not (so) my Lord. 2. If I have

found grace in Thy sight, first take my spirit that I
may go to my fathers and not behold the destruction
of my mother. 3. For two things vehemently con-
strain me : for I cannot resist Thee, and my soul,
moreover, cannot behold the evils of my mother.
4. But one thing I will say in Thy presence, O Lord.
5. What, therefore, will there be after these things?
for if Thou destroyest Thy city, and deliverest up
Thy land to those that hate us, how shall the name
of Israel be again remembered? 6. Or how shall
one speak of Thy praises? or to whom shall that
which is in Thy Law be explained? 7. Or shall
the world return to its nature (of aforetime), and
the age revert to primeval silence? 8. And shall the
multitude of souls be **taken away,** and the nature
of man not again be named? 9. And where is all
that which Thou didst say to Moses regarding us? "
    IV. And the Lord said unto me :
    " This city shall be delivered up for a time,
        And the people shall be chastened during a
        time,
        And the world shall not be given over to
        oblivion.

IV. 2–7. **The Heavenly Jerusalem.**

    2. [Dost thou think that this is a city of which I
said : ' On the palms of My hands have I graven
thee '? 3. This building now built in your midst is
not that which is revealed with Me ; that which was
prepared beforehand here from the time when I
took counsel to make Paradise, and showed it to
Adam before he sinned, but when he transgressed
the commandment, it was removed from him, as
also Paradise. 4. And after these things I showed
it to My servant Abraham by night among the
portions of the victims. 5. And again also I showed
it to Moses on Mount Sinai when I showed to him
the likeness of the tabernacle and all its vessels.
6. And now, behold, it is preserved with Me, as also

Paradise.   7. Go, therefore, and do as I command thee."]

V. 1–7. Baruch's Complaint, and God's Reassurance.

V. And I answered and said :
" So then I am destined **to grieve** for Zion,
    For Thine enemies will come to this place and
      pollute Thy sanctuary,
    And lead Thine inheritance into captivity,
    And make themselves masters of those whom
      Thou hast loved ;
    And they will depart again to the place of their
      idols,
    And will boast before them.
    And what wilt Thou do for **Thy** great name ? "
2.   And the Lord said unto me :
" My name and My glory have an eternal duration ;
    And My judgement shall maintain its right in
      its own time.
3. And thou shalt see with thine eyes
    That the enemy will not overthrow Zion,
    Nor burn Jerusalem,
    But be the ministers of the Judge for the time.
4. But do thou go and do whatsoever I have said
    unto thee."
5. And I went and took Jeremiah, and Adu, and Seriah, and Jabish, and Gedaliah, and all the honourable men of the people, and I led them to the valley of Cedron, and I narrated to them all that had been said to me.   6. And they lifted up their voice, and they all wept.   7. And we sat there and fasted until the evening.

VI. 1–VIII. 5. Invasion of the Chaldæans.

VI. And it came to pass on the morrow that, lo ! the army of the Chaldees surrounded the city, and at the time of the evening I, Baruch, left the people, and

I went forth and stood by the oak. 2. And I was
grieving over Zion, and lamenting over the captivity
which had come upon the people. 3. And, lo ! suddenly a strong spirit raised me, and bore me aloft
over the wall of Jerusalem. 4. And I beheld, and
lo ! four angels standing at the four corners of the
city, each of them holding a torch of fire in his
hands. 5. And another angel began to descend from
heaven, and said unto them : " Hold your lamps,
and do not light them till I tell you. 6. For I am
first sent to speak a word to the earth, and to place
in it what the Lord the Most High hath commanded
me." 7. And I saw him descend into the Holy of
Holies, and take from thence the veil, and the holy
ark, and the mercy-seat, and the two tables, and
the holy raiment of the priests, and the **altar of
incense,** and the forty-eight precious stones, wherewith the priest was adorned, and all the holy vessels
of the tabernacle. 8. And he spake to the earth
with a loud voice :

> " Earth, earth, earth, hear the word of the mighty
> God,
>> And receive what I commit to thee,
>> And guard thou them until the last times,
>> So that, when thou art ordered, thou mayst
>> restore them,
>> So that strangers may not get possession of
>> them.
> 9. For the time cometh when Jerusalem also shall
>> be delivered up for a time,
>> Until it is said, that it is again restored for
>> ever.
> 10. And the earth opened its mouth and swallowed
>> them up."

VII. And after these things I heard that angel
saying unto those angels who held the lamps :

> " Destroy, therefore, and overthrow its walls to
>> its foundations, lest the enemy should boast
>> and say :
>> ' We have overthrown the wall of Zion,

And we have burnt the place of the mighty
God.' "

2. And ye have seized the place where I had been
standing before.

VIII. Now the angels did as he had commanded
them, and when they had broken up the corners of
the walls, a voice was heard from the interior of the
temple, after the wall had fallen, saying :

2. " Enter, ye enemies,
    And come, ye adversaries ;
    For He Who kept the house hath forsaken (it)."

3. And I, Baruch, departed.   4. And it came to
pass after these things that the army of the Chaldees
entered and seized the house, and all that was
around it.   5. And they led the people away captive, and slew some of them, and bound Zedekiah
the king, and sent him to the king of Babylon.

IX. 1–XII. 4.   **First Fast.   Baruch's Dirge over Jerusalem.**

IX. And I, Baruch, came, and Jeremiah, whose
heart was found pure from sins, who had not been
captured in the seizure of the city.   2. And we rent
our garments, and wept, and mourned, and fasted
seven days.

X. And it came to pass after seven days, that the
word of God came to me, and said unto me :   2. " Tell
Jeremiah to go and support the captivity of the
people unto Babylon.   3. But do thou remain here
amid the desolation of Zion, and I will show to thee
after these days what will befall at the end of days."
4. And I said to Jeremiah as the Lord commanded
me.   5. And he, indeed, departed with the people,
but I, Baruch, returned and sat before the gates
of the temple, and I lamented with the following
lamentation over Zion and said :

6. " Blessed is he who was not born,
    Or being born hath died.

7. But as for us who live, woe unto us,

Because we see the afflictions of Zion,
And what hath befallen Jerusalem.

8. I will call the Sirens from the sea,
And ye Lilin, come ye from the desert,
And ye Shedim and dragons from the forests :
Awake and gird your loins unto mourning,
And take up with me the dirges,
And mourn with me.

9. Ye husbandmen, sow not again ;
And thou, earth, wherefore givest thou the
fruits of thy produce ?
Keep within thee the sweets of thy sustenance.

10. And thou, vine, why further dost thou give thy
wine ?
For an offering shall not again be made therefrom
in Zion,
Nor shall first-fruits again be offered.

11. And do ye, O heavens, withhold your dew,
And open not the treasuries of rain ;

12. And do thou, O sun, withhold the light of thy
rays ;
And do thou, O moon, extinguish the multitude
of thy light ;
For why should light rise again
Where the light of Zion is darkened ?

13. And you, ye bridegrooms, enter not in,
And let not the brides adorn themselves with
garlands ;
And, ye women, pray not that ye may bear.

14. For the barren shall rejoice more,
And those who have no sons shall be glad,
And those who have sons shall have anguish

15. For why should they bear in pain
Only to bury in grief ?

16. Or wherefore, again, should mankind have sons ;
Or wherefore should the seed of their nature
again be named,
Where this mother is desolate,
And her sons are led into captivity ?

17. From this time forward speak not of beauty,

And discourse not of gracefulness.

18. Moreover, ye priests, take ye the keys of the sanctuary,
And cast them into the height of heaven,
And give them to the Lord, and say :
' Guard Thy house Thyself,
For lo ! we are found false stewards.'

19. And you, ye virgins, who spin fine linen
And silk with gold of Ophir,
Hasten and take all things
And cast (them) into the fire,
That it may bear them to Him Who made them,
And the flame send them to Him Who created them,
Lest the enemy get possession of them."

XI. Moreover, I, Baruch, say this against thee, Babylon :

" If thou hadst prospered,
And Zion had dwelt in her glory,
It would have been a great grief to us
That thou shouldst be equal to Zion.

2. But now, lo ! the grief is infinite,
And the lamentation measureless,
For lo ! thou art prospered
And Zion desolate.

3. Who will be judge regarding these things ?
Or to whom shall we complain regarding that which hath befallen us ?
O Lord, how hast Thou borne (it) ?

4. Our fathers went to rest without grief,
And lo ! the righteous sleep in the earth in tranquillity ;

5. For they knew not this anguish,
Nor yet had they heard of that which had befallen us.

6. Would that thou hadst ears, O earth,
And that thou hadst a heart, O dust,
That ye might go and announce in Sheol,
And say to the dead :

7. ' Blessed are ye more than we who live.' "

XII. But I will say this as I think;
  And I will speak against thee, O land, which
    art prospering.
2. The noonday doth not always burn;
  Nor do the constant rays of the sun always give
    light.
3. Do not expect [and hope] that thou wilt always
    be prosperous and rejoicing;
  And be not greatly uplifted and **boastful;**
4. For assuredly in its own season wrath will
    awake against thee,
  Which now in long-suffering is held in as it
    were by reins.

XII. 5–XIII. 12. **Second Fast.   Judgement on the Heathen.**

5. And when I had said these things, I fasted
    seven days.
XIII. And it came to pass after these things, that
I, Baruch, was standing upon Mount Zion, and lo!
a voice came from the height and said unto me:
2. "Stand upon thy feet, Baruch, and hear the word
of the mighty God.   3. Because thou hast been
astonied at what hath befallen Zion, thou shalt therefore be assuredly preserved to the consummation of
the times, that thou mayst be a testimony.   4. So
that, if ever those prosperous cities say: ' Why hath
the mighty God brought upon us this retribution? '
5. Say thou to them, thou and those like thee who
shall have seen this evil: ' ⟨This is the evil⟩ and
retribution which is coming upon you and upon your
people in its (destined) time, that the nations may
be thoroughly **smitten.**'   6. And **they shall be in
anguish.**   7. And if they say at that time: **'For
how long?'**   8. Thou shalt say to them:
  ' Ye who have drunk the strained wine,
    Drink ye also of its dregs,
    The judgement of the Lofty One
    Who hath no respect of persons.'

9. On this account He had before no mercy on
   His own sons,
   But afflicted them as His enemies, because they
   sinned.
10. They were, therefore, chastened then
   That they might be sanctified.
11. But now, ye peoples and nations, ye are
   guilty,
   Because all this time ye have trodden down the
   earth,
   And used the creation unrighteously.
12. For I have always benefited you;
   And ye have always been ungrateful for the
   beneficence."

XIV. 1–XIX. 8. God's Judgements are incomprehensible.

XIV. And I answered and said : " Lo ! Thou hast
shown me the method of the times, and that which
shall be after these things, and Thou hast said unto
me, that the retribution, which hath been spoken of
by Thee, shall come upon the nations. 2. And now
I know that those who have sinned are many, and
they have lived in prosperity, and departed from the
world, but that few nations will be left in those
times, to whom those words shall be said which
Thou didst say. 3. For what advantage is there in
this, or what (evil), worse than what we have seen
befall us, are we to expect to see? 4. But again I
will speak in Thy presence : 5. What have they
profited who had knowledge before Thee, and have
not walked in vanity as the rest of the nations, and
have not said to the dead : ' Give us life,' but
always feared Thee, and have not left Thy ways?
6. And lo ! they have been carried off; nor on their
account hast Thou had mercy on Zion. 7. And if
others did evil, it was due to Zion, that on account
of the works of those who wrought good works she
should be forgiven, and should not be overwhelmed

on account of the works of those who wrought unrighteousness.

8. But who, O LORD, my Lord, will comprehend Thy judgement,

Or who will search out the profoundness of Thy path?

Or who will think out the weight of Thy way?

9. Or who will be able to think out Thy incomprehensible counsel?

Or who of those that are born hath found

The beginning or end of Thy wisdom?

10. For we have all been made like a breath. 11. For as the breath ascends involuntarily, and again dies, so it is with the nature of men, who depart not according to their own will, and know not what will befall them in the end. 12. For the righteous justly hope for the end, and without fear depart from this habitation, because they have with Thee a store of works preserved in treasuries. 13. On this account also these without fear leave this world, and trusting with joy they hope to receive the world which Thou hast promised them. 14. But as for us,—woe to us, who also are now shamefully entreated, and at that time look forward (only) to evils. 15. But Thou knowest accurately what Thou hast done by means of Thy servants; for we are not able to understand that which is good as Thou art, our Creator. 16. But again I will speak in Thy presence, O LORD, my Lord. 17. When of old there was no world with its inhabitants, Thou didst devise and speak with a word, and forthwith the works of creation stood before Thee. 18. And Thou didst say that Thou wouldst make for Thy world man as the administrator of Thy works, that it might be known that he was by no means made on account of the world, but the world on account of him. 19. And now I see that as for the world which was made on account of us, lo! it abideth, but we, on account of whom it was made, depart."

XV. And the Lord answered and said unto me:

" Thou art rightly astonied regarding the departure of man ; but thou hast not judged well regarding the evils which befall those who sin.   2. And as regards what thou hast said, that the righteous are carried off and the impious are prospered,   3. And as regards what thou hast said : ' Man knoweth not Thy judgement '—4. On this account hear, and I will speak to thee, and hearken, and I will cause thee to hear My words.   5. Man would not rightly have understood My judgement, if he had not accepted the Law, and I had not instructed him in understanding.   6. But now, because he transgressed wittingly, yea, just on this ground that he wot thereof, he shall be tormented. 7. And as regards what thou didst say touching the righteous, that on account of them hath this world come, so also again **shall** that which is to come **come** on their account.   8. For this world is to them a strife and a labour with much trouble ; and that accordingly which is to come, a crown with great glory."

XVI. And I answered and said : " O LORD, my Lord, lo ! the years of this time are few and evil, and who is able in **his** little **time** to acquire that which is measureless ? "

XVII. And the Lord answered and said unto me : " With the Most High account is not taken of much time nor of a few years.   2. For what did it profit Adam that he lived nine hundred and thirty years, and transgressed that which he was commanded ?   3. Therefore the multitude of time that he lived did not profit him, but brought death and cut off the years of those who were born from him.   4. Or wherein did Moses suffer loss in that he lived only one hundred and twenty years, and, inasmuch as he was subject to Him Who formed him, brought the Law to the seed of Jacob, and lighted a lamp for the nation of Israel ? "

XVIII. And I answered and said : " He that lighted hath taken from the light, and there are but few that have imitated him.   2. But those many

whom He hath lighted have taken from the darkness
of Adam, and have not rejoiced in the light of the
lamp."

XIX. And He answered and said unto me :
" Wherefore at that time he appointed for them a
covenant, and said :

 ' Behold I have placed before you life and death,
  And he called heaven and earth to witness
   against them.
 2. For he knew that his time was but short,
  But that heaven and earth endure always.
 3. But after his death they sinned and transgressed,
  Though they knew that they had the **Law**
   reproving (them),
  And the light in which nothing could err,
  Also the spheres, which testify, and Me.

4. Now regarding everything that is, it is I that
judge, but do not thou take counsel in thy soul
regarding these things, nor afflict thyself because of
those which have been. 5. For now it is the consummation of time that should be considered, whether
of business, or of prosperity, or of shame, and not
the beginning thereof. 6. Because if a man be prospered in his beginnings and shamefully entreated in
his old age, he forgetteth all the prosperity that he
had. 7. And again, if a man is shamefully entreated
in his beginnings, and at his end is prospered, he
remembereth not again his evil entreatment. 8. And
again hearken : though each one were prospered all
that time—all the time from the day on which
death was decreed against those who transgress—and
in his end was destroyed, in vain would have been
everything."

XX. 1–6. The Advent of the Judgement.

XX. Therefore, behold ! the days will come,
 And the times will hasten more than the former,
 And the seasons will speed on more than those
  that are past,

And the years will pass more quickly than the
present (years).

2. Therefore have I now taken away Zion,
That I may the more speedily visit the world
in its season.

3. Now, therefore, hold fast in thy heart everything
that I command thee,
And seal it in the recesses of thy mind.

4. And then I will show thee the judgement of My
might,
And My ways which are past finding out.

5. Go, therefore, and sanctify thyself seven days,
and eat no bread, nor drink water, nor speak to any
one. 6. And afterwards come to that place, and I
will reveal Myself to thee, and speak true things with
thee, and I will give thee commandment regarding
the method of the times; for they are coming and
tarry not.

XXI. 1–26. The Prayer of Baruch, the Son of Neriah.

XXI. And I went thence and sat in the valley of
Cedron in a cave of the earth, and I sanctified my
soul there, and I ate no bread, yet I was not hungry,
and I drank no water, yet I thirsted not, and I was
there till the seventh day, as He had commanded
me. 2. And afterwards I came to that place where
He had spoken with me. 3. And it came to pass
at sunset that my soul took much thought, and I
began to speak in the presence of the Mighty One,
and said : 4. " O Thou that hast made the earth,
hear me, that hast fixed the firmament **by the word,**
and hast made firm the height of the heaven by the
spirit, that hast called from the beginning of the
world that which did not yet exist, and they obey
Thee. 5. Thou that hast commanded the air by
Thy nod, and hast seen those things which are to be
as those things which Thou art doing. 6. Thou that
rulest with great thought the powers that stand

before Thee : (yea) that rulest with indignation the
holy living creatures, who are without number, which
Thou didst make from the beginning, of flame and
fire, which stand around Thy throne.   7. To Thee
only doth this belong that Thou shouldst do forthwith whatsoever Thou dost wish.   8. Who causest
the drops of rain to rain by number upon the earth,
and alone knowest the consummation of the times
before they come : have respect unto my prayer.
9. For Thou alone art able to sustain all who are,
and those who **have** passed away, and those who are
to be, those who sin, and those who **are righteous**
[as living (and) being past finding out].   10. For Thou
alone dost live immortal and art past finding out,
and knowest the number of mankind.   11. And if in
time many have sinned, yet others, not a few, have
been righteous.

XXI. 12–18. **Baruch's Depreciation of this Life.**

12. Thou knowest where Thou preservest the end
of those who have sinned, or the consummation of
those who have been righteous.   13. For if there
were this life only, which belongeth to all men,
nothing could be more bitter than this.

14. For of what profit is strength that turneth to
weakness,

Or **fulness of food** that turneth to famine,

Or beauty that turneth to ugliness?

15. For the nature of man is always changeable.
16. For what we were formerly we now no longer
are, and what we now are we shall not afterwards
remain.   17. For if a consummation had been prepared for all, in vain would have been their beginning.   18. But regarding everything that cometh from
Thee, do Thou inform me, and regarding everything
about which I ask Thee, do Thou enlighten me.

XXI. 19–26. **Baruch prayeth to God to hasten the Judgement.**

19. How long will that which is corruptible remain, and how long will the time of mortals be prospered, and until what time will those who transgress in the world be polluted with much wickedness? 20. Command therefore in mercy, and accomplish all that Thou saidst Thou wouldst bring, that Thy might may be made known to those who think that Thy long-suffering is weakness. 21. And show to those who know not, **that** everything that hath befallen us and our city until now **hath been** according to the long-suffering of Thy power; because on account of Thy name Thou hast called us a beloved people. 22. Bring to an end, therefore, henceforth mortality. 23. And reprove, accordingly, the angel of death, and let Thy glory appear, and let the might of Thy beauty be known, and let Sheol be sealed so that from this time forward it may not receive the dead, and let the treasuries of souls restore those which are enclosed in them. 24. For there have been many years like those that are desolate from the days of Abraham and Isaac and Jacob, and of all those who are like them, who sleep in the earth, on whose account Thou didst say that Thou hadst created the world. 25. And now quickly show Thy glory, and do not defer what hath been promised by Thee." 26. And ⟨when⟩ I had completed the words of this prayer I was greatly weakened.

XXII. 1–XXIII. 7. **God's Reply to Baruch's Prayer.**

XXII. And it came to pass after these things that lo! the heavens were opened, and I saw, and power was given to me, and a voice was heard from on high, and it said unto me : 2. " Baruch, Baruch, why art thou troubled? 3. He who travelleth by a road but doth not complete it, or he who departeth by sea but

D

doth not arrive at the port, can he be comforted?
4. Or he who promiseth to give a present to another,
but doth not fulfil it, is it not robbery? 5. Or he
who soweth the earth, but doth not reap its fruit in
its season, doth he not lose everything? 6. Or he
who planteth a plant, unless it groweth till the time
suitable to it, doth he who planted it expect to
receive fruit from it? 7. Or a woman who hath
conceived, if she bring forth untimely, doth she not
assuredly slay her infant? 8. Or he who buildeth a
house, if he doth not roof it and complete it, can it
be called a house? Tell me that first."

XXIII. And I answered and said: "Not so, O
LORD, my Lord." 2. And He answered and said
unto me: "Why therefore art thou troubled about
that which thou knowest not, and why art thou ill
at ease about things in which thou art ignorant?
3. For as thou hast not forgotten the people who
now are and those who have passed away, so I
remember those who **are appointed** to come. 4. Because when Adam sinned and death was decreed
against those who should be born, then the multitude of those who should be born was numbered,
and for that number a place was prepared where the
living might dwell and the dead might be guarded.
5. **Before,** therefore, the number aforesaid is fulfilled,
the creature will not live again [for My spirit is the
creator of life], and Sheol shall receive the dead.
6. And, again, it is given to thee to hear what things
are to come after these times. 7. For truly My
redemption hath drawn nigh, and is not far distant
as aforetime.

XXIV. 1–4. **The Coming Judgement.**

XXIV. " For behold ! the days come and the books
shall be opened in which are written the sins of all
those who have sinned ; and, again, also the treasuries
in which the righteousness of all those who have been
righteous in creation is gathered. 2. For it shall

come to pass at that time that thou shalt see—and many that are with thee—the long-suffering of the Most High, which hath been throughout all generations, Who hath been long-suffering towards all who are born, (alike) those who sin and (those who) are righteous." 3. And I answered and said: "But, behold! O Lord, no one knoweth the number of those things which have passed, nor yet of those things which are to come. 4. For I know, indeed, that which hath befallen us, but what will happen to our enemies I know not; and when Thou wilt visit Thy works."

XXV. 1–XXVI. 1. The Sign of the Coming Judgement.

XXV. And He answered and said unto me: "Thou, too, shalt be preserved till that time, till that sign which the Most High will work for the inhabitants of the earth in the end of days. 2. This, therefore, shall be the sign. 3. When a stupor shall seize the inhabitants of the earth, and they shall fall into many tribulations, and again, when they shall fall into great torments. 4. And it shall come to pass when they say in their thoughts by reason of their much tribulation: 'The Mighty One doth no longer remember the earth'—yea, it will come to pass when they abandon hope, that the time will then awake."

XXVI. And I answered and said: "Will that tribulation which is to be continue a long time, and will that necessity embrace many years?"

XXVII. 1–XXX. 1. The Twelve Woes: the Messiah and the temporary Messianic Kingdom.

XXVII. And He answered and said unto me: "Into twelve parts is that time divided, and each one of them is reserved for that which is appointed

for it.   2. In the first part there shall be the beginning
of commotions.   3. And in the second part (there
shall be) slayings of the great ones.   4. And in the
third part the fall of many by death.   5. And in
the fourth part the sending of the sword.   6. And
in the fifth part famine and the withholding of rain.
7. And in the sixth part earthquakes and terrors.
8. [Wanting.]   9. And in the eighth part a multitude
of spectres and attacks of the Shedim.   10. And in
the ninth part the fall of fire.   11. And in the tenth
part rapine and much oppression.   12. And in the
eleventh part wickedness and unchastity.   13. And
in the twelfth part confusion from the mingling
together of all those things aforesaid.   14. For these
parts of that time are reserved, and shall be mingled
one with another and minister one to another.
15. For some shall **leave out** some of their own, and
receive (in its stead) from others; and some shall
complete their own and that of others, so that those
may not understand who are upon the earth in those
days that this is the consummation of the times.

XXVIII. " Nevertheless, whosoever understandeth
shall then be wise.   2. For the measure and reckoning of that time are two parts a week of seven weeks."
3. And I answered and said : " It is good for a man
to come and behold, but it is better that he should
not come lest he fall.   4. [But I will say this also.
5. ' Will he who is incorruptible despise those things
which are corruptible, and whatever befalleth in the
case of those things which are corruptible, so that he
might look only to those things which are not corruptible ? ']   6. But if, O Lord, those things shall
assuredly come to pass which Thou hast foretold to
me ; so do Thou show this also unto me if, indeed, I
have found grace in Thy sight.   7. Is it in one
place or in one of the parts of the earth that those
things are to come to pass, or will the whole earth
experience (them) ? "

XXIX. And He answered and said unto me :
" Whatever shall then befall (shall befall) the whole

earth; therefore all who live shall experience (them).
2. For at that time I will protect only those who are
found in those self-same days in this land.   3. And
it shall come to pass when all is accomplished that
was to come to pass in those parts, that the Messiah
shall then begin to be revealed.   4. And Behemoth
shall be revealed from his place, and Leviathan shall
ascend from the sea, those two great monsters which
I created on the fifth day of creation, and shall have
kept until that time; and then they shall be for
food for all that are left.   5. The earth also shall
yield its fruit ten thousandfold, and on one vine there
shall be a thousand branches, and each branch shall
produce a thousand clusters, and each cluster shall
produce a thousand grapes, and each grape shall produce a cor of wine.   6. And those who have hungered
shall rejoice; moreover, also, they shall behold
marvels every day.   7. For winds shall go forth
from before Me to bring every morning the fragrance
of aromatic fruits, and at the close of the day clouds
distilling the dew of health.   8. And it shall come
to pass at that self-same time that the treasury of
manna shall again descend from on high, and they
shall eat of it in those years, because these are they
who have come to the consummation of time.

XXX. "And it shall come to pass after these
things, when the time of the advent of the Messiah
is fulfilled, and He shall return in glory.

XXX. 2–5. The Resurrection.

2. Then shall all who have fallen asleep in hope
of Him rise again.   And it shall come to pass at that
time that the treasuries shall be opened in which is
preserved the number of the souls of the righteous,
and they shall come forth, and a multitude of souls
shall be seen together in one assemblage of one
thought, and the first shall rejoice and the last shall
not be grieved.   3. For **they know** that the time
hath come of which it is said, that it is the

consummation of the times.   4. But the souls of the wicked, when they behold all these things, shall then waste away the more.   5. For they shall know that their torment .hath come and their perdition hath arrived."

XXXI.–XXXIII. Baruch's Exhortation to the People.

XXXI. And it came to pass after these things that I went to the people and said unto them : " Assemble unto me all your elders and I will speak words unto them." 2. And they all assembled in the valley of the Cedron. 3. And I answered and said unto them :

" Hear, O Israel, and I will speak to thee,
　　And give ear, O seed of Jacob, and I will
　　　instruct thee.
4. Forget not Zion,
　　But hold in remembrance the anguish of Jerusalem.
5. For lo ! the days come,
　　When everything that existeth will become the
　　　prey of corruption,
　　And be as though it had not been.

XXXII. " But as for you, if ye prepare your hearts, so as to sow in them the fruits of the Law, it shall protect you in that time in which the Mighty One is to shake the whole creation. [2. Because after a little time the building of Zion shall be shaken in order that it may again be built. 3. But that building shall not remain, but shall again after a time be rooted out, and shall remain desolate until the time. 4. And afterwards it must be renewed in glory, and perfected for evermore.] 5. Therefore we should not **be distressed** so much over the evil which hath now come as over that which is still to be. 6. For there shall be a greater trial than these two tribulations when the Mighty One shall renew His creation.

7. And now do not draw near to me for a few days,
nor seek me till I come to you." 8. And it came
to pass when I had spoken to them all these words,
that I, Baruch, went my way; and when the people
saw me setting out, they lifted up their voice and
lamente1 and said: 9. "Whither departest thou
from us, Baruch, and forsakest us as a father who
forsaketh his orphan children, and departeth from
them?

XXXIII. "Are these the commands which thy
companion, Jeremiah the prophet, commanded thee,
and said unto thee: 2. 'Look to this people till
I go and make ready the rest of the brethren in
Babylon, against whom hath gone forth the sentence
that they should be led into captivity?' 3. And
now if thou also forsake us, it were good for us all
to die before thee, and then that thou shouldst
withdraw from us."

XXXIV.–XXXV. Baruch's Lament.

XXXIV. And I answered and said unto the
people: "Far be it from me to forsake you or to
withdraw from you, but I will only go unto the
Holy of Holies to enquire of the Mighty One concerning you and concerning Zion, if in some respect
I should receive more illumination; and after these
things I will return to you."

XXXV. And I, Baruch, went to the holy place,
and sat down upon the ruins and wept, and said:

2. "O that mine eyes were springs,
   And ye, mine eyelids a fount of tears.

3. For how shall I lament for Zion,
   And how shall I mourn for Jerusalem?

4. For in that place where I am now prostrate;
   The high priest of old offered holy sacrifices,
   And placed thereon incense of fragrant odours.

5. But now our glorying hath been made into dust,
   And the desire of our soul into sand."

XXXVI.–XXXVII. **The Vision of the Forest.**

XXXVI. And when I had said these things I fell asleep there, and I saw a vision in the night. 2. And lo ! a forest of trees planted on the plain, and lofty and rugged rocky mountains surrounded it, and that forest occupied much space. 3. And lo ! over against it arose a vine, and from under it there went forth a fountain peacefully. 4. Now that fountain came to the forest and was (stirred) into great waves, and those waves submerged that forest, and suddenly they rooted out the greater part of that forest, and overthrew all the mountains which were round about it. 5. And the height of the forest began to be made low, and the top of the mountains was made low, and that fountain prevailed greatly, so that it left nothing of that great forest save one cedar only. 6. Also when it had cast it down and had destroyed and rooted out the greater part of that forest, so that nothing was left of it, nor could its place be recognised, then that vine began to come with the fountain in peace and great tranquillity, and it came to a place which was not far from the cedar, and they brought the cedar which had been cast down to it. 7. And I beheld and lo ! that vine opened its mouth and spake and said to that cedar : "Art thou not that cedar which was left of the forest of wickedness, and by whose means wickedness persisted, and was wrought all those years, and goodness never ? 8. And thou didst keep conquering that which was not thine, and to that which was thine thou didst never show compassion, and thou didst keep extending thy power over those who were far from thee, and those who drew nigh thee thou didst hold fast in the toils of thy wickedness, and thou didst uplift thyself always as one that could not be rooted out ! 9. But now thy time hath sped and thine hour is come. 10. Do thou also, therefore, depart, O cedar, after the forest, which departed before thee, and become dust with it, and let your ashes be mingled together. 11. And now recline in anguish and rest in torment till thy last time come, in which thou shalt come again, and be tormented still more."

XXXVII. And after these things I saw that cedar burning, and the vine growing, itself and all around it, (but) the plain full of unfading flowers. And I, indeed, awoke and arose.

XXXVIII.–XL. The Interpretation of the Vision.

XXXVIII. And I prayed and said : " O LORD, my Lord, Thou dost always enlighten those who are led by understanding. 2. Thy Law is life, and Thy wisdom is right guidance. 3. Make known to me, therefore, the interpretation of this vision. 4. For Thou knowest that my soul hath always walked in Thy Law, and from my (earliest) days I departed not from Thy wisdom."

XXXIX. And He answered and said unto me : " Baruch, this is the interpretation of the vision which thou hast seen. 2. As thou hast seen a great forest which lofty and rugged mountains surrounded, this is the word. 3. Behold ! the days come, and this kingdom shall be destroyed which once destroyed Zion, and it shall be subjected to that which cometh after it. 4. Moreover, that also, again, after a time shall be destroyed, and another, a third, shall arise; and that also shall have dominion for its time, and shall be destroyed. 5. And after these things a fourth kingdom shall arise, whose power shall be harsh and evil far beyond those which were before it, and it shall rule many times as the forests on the plain, and it shall hold fast the times, and shall exalt itself more than the cedars of Lebanon. 6. And by it the truth shall be hidden, and all those who are polluted with iniquity shall flee to it, as evil beasts flee and creep into the forest. 7. And it shall come to pass when the time of his consummation that he should fall hath approached, then the **principate** of My Messiah shall be revealed, which is like the fountain and the vine; and when it is revealed it shall root out the multitude of its host. 8. And as touching that which thou hast seen, the lofty cedar, which was left of that forest, and the fact that the vine spoke those words with it which thou didst hear, this is the word:

XL. The last leader of that time shall be left alive, when the multitude of his hosts shall be put to the sword, and he shall be bound, and they shall take him up to Mount Zion, and My Messiah shall convict him of all his impieties, and shall gather and set before him all the works of his hosts. 2. And afterwards he shall put him to death, and protect the rest of My people which shall be found in the place which I have chosen. 3. And his principate shall stand for ever, until the world of corruption is at an end, and until the times aforesaid are fulfilled. 4. This is thy vision, and this is its interpretation."

XLI.–XLII. The Destiny of the Apostates and Proselytes.

XLI. And I answered and said : " To whom and for many shall these things be? Or who will be worthy to live at that time? 2. For I will speak before Thee everything that I think, and I will ask of Thee regarding those things which I meditate. 3. For lo! I see many of Thy people who have withdrawn from Thy covenant, and cast from them the yoke of Thy Law. 4. But others, again, I have seen who have forsaken their vanity, and fled for refuge beneath Thy wings. 5. What, therefore, shall be to them? Or how shall the last time receive them? 6. Or perhaps the time of these shall assuredly be weighed, and as the beam inclineth shall they be judged accordingly? "

XLII. And He answered and said unto me :

" These things also I will show unto thee. 2. As
for what thou didst say: ' To whom shall these things
be, and how many (shall they be) ? '—to those who
have believed there shall be the good which was
spoken of aforetime, and to those who despise there
shall be the contrary of these things. 3. And as
for what thou didst say regarding those who have
drawn near and those who have withdrawn, this is
the word: 4. As for those who were before subject,
and afterwards withdrew and mingled themselves
with the seed of mingled peoples, the time of these
was the former, and was accounted as something
exalted. 5. And as for those who before knew not,
but afterwards knew life, and mingled (only) with
the seed of the **people** which had separated itself,
the time of these (is) the **latter,** and is accounted
as something exalted. 6. And time shall succeed
to time and season to season, and one shall receive
from another, and then with a view to the consummation shall everything be compared according to
the measure of the times and the hours of the seasons.
7. For corruption shall take those that belong to it,
and life those that belong to it. 8. And the dust
shall be called, and there shall be said to it : ' Give
back that which is not thine, and raise up all that
thou hast kept until its time.'

XLIII. **Baruch is told of his Death.**

XLIII. " But, do thou, Baruch, direct thy heart
    for that which hath been said to thee,
    And understand those things which have been
      shown to thee ;
    For there are many eternal consolations for thee.
  2. For thou shalt depart from this place,
    And thou shalt pass from the regions which
      are now seen by thee,
    And thou shalt forget whatever is corruptible,
    And shalt not again recall those things which
      happen among mortals.

3. Go therefore and command thy people, and
come to this place, and afterwards fast seven
days, and then I will come to thee and speak
with thee."

XLIV.–XLVII. **Baruch's Words to the People.**

XLIV. And I, Baruch, went from thence, and
came to my people, and I called my first-born son
and [the Gedaliahs] my friends, and seven of the
elders of the people, and I said unto them :

2. " Behold, I go unto my fathers
According to the way of all the earth.

3. But withdraw ye not from the way of the Law,
But guard and admonish the people which remain,
Lest they withdraw from the commandments
of the Mighty One.

4. For ye see that He Whom we serve is just,
And our Creator is no respecter of persons.

5. And ye see what hath befallen Zion,
And what hath happened to Jerusalem.

6. For the judgement of the Mighty One shall
(thereby) be made known,
And His ways, which, though past finding out,
are right.

7. For if ye endure and persevere in His fear,
And do not forget His Law,
The times shall change over you for good,
And ye shall see the consolation of Zion.

8. Because whatever is now is nothing,
But that which shall be is very great.

9. For everything that is corruptible shall pass
away,
And everything that dieth shall depart,
And all the present time shall be forgotten,
Nor shall there be any remembrance of the
present time, which is defiled with evils.

10. For that which runneth now runneth unto vanity,
And that which prospereth shall quickly fall
and be humiliated.

11. For that which is to be shall be the object of
desire,
    And on that which shall come afterwards do
    we place our hope;
    For it is a time that shall not pass away.

12. And the hour cometh which shall abide for ever,
    And the new world (cometh) which doth not
    turn to corruption those who depart **to its
    blessedness,**
    And hath no mercy on those who depart to
    torment,
    And shall not lead to perdition those who live
    in it.

13. For these are they who shall inherit that time
    which hath been spoken of,
    And theirs is the inheritance of the promised
    time.

14. These are they who have acquired for themselves
    treasures of wisdom,
    And with them are found stores of under-
    standing,
    And from mercy have they not withdrawn,
    And the truth of the Law have they preserved.

15. For to them shall be given the world to come.
    But the dwelling of the rest, who are many, shall
    be in the fire.

XLV. " Do ye, therefore, so far as ye are able,
instruct the people, for that labour is yours.   2. For
if ye teach them, ye will quicken them."

XLVI. And my son and the elders of the people
answered and said unto me :
    " Hath the Mighty One humiliated us to such
    a degree
    As to take thee from us quickly?

2. And truly we shall be in darkness,
    And there will be no light to the people who
    are left.

3. For where again shall we seek the Law,
    Or who will distinguish for us between death
    and life? "

4. And I said unto them : " The throne of the
   Mighty One I cannot resist :
   Nevertheless, there shall not be wanting to
   Israel a wise man,
   Nor a son of the Law to the race of Jacob.

5. But only prepare ye your hearts, that ye may
   obey the Law,
   And be subject to those who in fear are wise
   and understanding ;
   And prepare your soul that ye may not depart
   from them.

6. For if ye do these things,
   Good tidings shall come unto you
[which I before told you of ; nor will ye fall into the
torment, of which I testified to you before."   7. But
with regard to the word that I was to be taken,
I did not make (it) known to them or to my son].

XLVII. And when I had gone forth and dismissed
them, I went thence and said unto them : " Behold !
I go to Hebron ; for thither the Mighty One hath
sent me."   2. And I came to that place where the
word had been spoken to me, and I sat there, and
fasted seven days.

XLVIII. 1–47. **Prayer of Baruch.**

XLVIII. And it came to pass after the seventh
day, that I prayed before the Mighty One and said :

2. " O my Lord, Thou summonest the advent of
   the times,
   And they stand before Thee ;
   Thou causest the power of the ages to pass away,
   And they do not resist Thee ;
   Thou arrangest the method of the seasons,
   And they obey Thee.

3. Thou alone knowest the duration of the generations,
   And Thou revealest not Thy mysteries to many.

4. Thou makest known the multitude of the fire,
   And Thou weighest the lightness of the wind.

5. Thou explorest the limit of the heights,
   And Thou scrutinisest the depths of the darkness.
6. Thou **carest for** the number which pass away
   that they may be preserved,
   And Thou preparest an abode for those that
   are to be.
7. Thou rememberest the beginning which Thou
   hast made,
   And the destruction that is to be Thou forgettest
   not.
8 With nods of fear and indignation Thou **givest**
   commandment to the flames,
   And they change into spirits,
   And with a word Thou quickenest that which
   was not,
   And with mighty power Thou holdest that
   which hath not yet come.
9. Thou instructest created things in the understanding of Thee,
   And Thou makest wise the spheres so as to
   minister in their orders.
10. Armies innumerable stand before Thee,
    And minister in their orders quietly at Thy nod.
11. Hear Thy servant,
    And give ear to my petition.
12. For in a little time are we born,
    And in a little time do we return.
13. But with Thee hours are as a time,
    And days as generations.
14. Be not therefore wroth with man; for he is
    nothing,
    And take not account of our works. 15. for
    what are we?
    For lo! by Thy gift do we come into the world,
    And we depart not of our own will.
16. For we said not to our parents, ' Beget us,'
    Nor did we send to Sheol and say, ' Receive
    us.'
17. What, therefore, is our strength that we should
    bear Thy wrath?

Or what are we that we should endure Thy
judgement?

18. Protect us in Thy compassions,
And in Thy mercy help us.

19. Behold the little ones that are subject unto Thee,
And save all that draw nigh unto Thee;
And destroy not the hope of our people,
And cut not short the times of our aid.

20. For this is the **nation** which Thou hast chosen,
And these are the people, to whom Thou findest
no equal.

21. But I will speak now before Thee,
And I will say as my heart thinketh.

22. In Thee do we trust, for lo ! Thy Law is with us,
And we know that we shall not fall so long as
we keep Thy statutes.

23. [To all times we are blessed; in this at least
that we have not mingled with the Gentiles.]

24. For we are all one celebrated people,
Who have received one Law from One;
And the Law which is amongst us will aid us,
And the surpassing wisdom which is in us will
help us."

25. And when I had prayed and said these things,
I was greatly weakened. 26. And He answered and
said unto me :

" Thou hast prayed simply, O Baruch,
And all thy words have been heard.

27. But My judgement exacteth its own,
And My Law exacteth its rights.

28. For from thy words I will answer thee,
And from thy prayer I will speak to thee.

29. For this is as followeth : he that is corrupted
is not at all; he hath both wrought iniquity so far
as he could do anything, and hath not remembered
My goodness, nor accepted My long-suffering. 30.
Therefore thou shalt surely be taken up, as I before
told thee. 31. For that time shall arise which
bringeth affliction; for it shall come and pass by
with quick vehemence, and it shall be turbulent,

coming in the heat of indignation.   32. And it shall
come to pass in those days that all the inhabitants
of the earth will **be moved** one against another,
because they know not that My judgement hath
drawn nigh.

33. For there shall not be found many wise at that
time,

And the intelligent shall be but a few :
Moreover, even those who know shall most of
all be silent.

34. And there shall be many rumours and tidings
not a few,

And the doings of phantasmata shall be manifest,
And promises not a few be recounted ;
Some of them (shall prove) idle,
And some of them shall be confirmed.

35. And honour shall be turned into shame,
And strength humiliated into contempt,
And probity destroyed,
And beauty shall become ugliness.

36. And many shall say to many at that time :
' Where hath the multitude of intelligence
hidden itself,

And whither hath the multitude of wisdom
removed itself ? '

37. And whilst they are meditating these things,
Then envy shall arise in those who had not
thought aught of themselves (?),

And passion shall seize him who is peaceful,
And many shall be roused in anger to injure
many,

And they shall raise up armies in order to shed
blood,

And in the end they shall perish together with
them.

38. And it shall come to pass at the self-same time,
That a change of times shall manifestly appear
to every man,

Because in all those times they polluted themselves,

E

And practised oppression,
And walked every man in his own works,
And remembered not the Law of the Mighty One.

39. Therefore a fire shall consume their thoughts,
And in flame shall the meditations of their reins
be tried;
For the Judge shall come and will not tarry.

40. Because each of the inhabitants of the earth
knew when he was committing iniquity,
And they have not known My Law by reason
of their pride.

41. But many shall then assuredly weep,
Yea, over the living more than over the dead."

42. And I answered and said :
" O Adam, what hast thou done to all those
who are born from thee ?
And what will be said to the first Eve who
hearkened to the serpent ?

43. For all this multitude is going to corruption,
Nor is there any numbering of those whom the
fire devoureth.

44. But again I will speak in Thy presence. 45.
Thou, O LORD, my Lord, knowest what is in Thy
creature. 46. For Thou didst of old command the
dust to produce Adam, and Thou knowest the
number of those who are born from him, and how
far they have sinned before Thee who have existed
and not confessed Thee as their Creator. 47. And
as regards all these their end will convict them, and
Thy Law which they have transgressed shall requite
them on Thy day."

XLVIII. 48–50. Fragment of an Address of Baruch to the People.

[48. " But now let us dismiss the wicked and enquire
about the righteous. 49. And I will recount their
blessedness, and not be silent in celebrating their
glory, which is reserved for them. 50. For assuredly
as in a little time in this world which passeth away,
in which ye live, ye have endured much labour, so

in that world to which there is no end, ye shall receive great light."]

XLIX.–LII. The Nature of the Resurrection Body; the final Destinies of the Righteous and of the Wicked.

XLIX. " Nevertheless, I will again ask from Thee, O Mighty One, yea, I will ask mercy from Him Who made all things :

2. ' In what shape will those live who live in Thy day?

Or how will the splendour of those who (are) after that time continue?

3. Will they then resume this form of the present, And put on these entrammeling members, Which are now involved in evils, And in which evils are consummated; Or wilt Thou perchance change these things which have been in the world, As also the world? ' "

L. And He answered and said unto me : " Hear, Baruch, this word,

And write in the remembrance of thy heart all that thou shalt learn.

2. For the earth shall then assuredly restore the dead, Which it now receiveth, in order to preserve them.

It shall make no change in their form, But as it hath received, so shall it restore them; And as I delivered them unto it, so also shall it raise them.

3. For then it will be necessary to show to the living that the dead have come to life again, and that those who had departed have returned (again). 4. And it shall come to pass, when they have severally recognized those whom they now know, then judgement shall grow strong, and those things which before were spoken of shall come.

LI. " And it shall come to pass, when that appointed day hath gone by, that then shall the **aspect**

of those who are condemned be afterwards changed,
and the glory of those who are justified. 2. For the
aspect of those who now act wickedly shall become
worse than it is, as they shall suffer torment. 3.
Also (as for) the glory of those who have now been
justified in My Law, who have had understanding
in their life, and who have planted in their heart
the root of wisdom, then their splendour shall be
glorified in changes, and the form of their face shall
be turned into the light of their beauty, that they
may be able to acquire and receive the world which
doth not die, which is then promised to them. 4. For
over this above all shall those who come then lament,
that they rejected My Law, and stopped their ears
that they might not hear wisdom or receive understanding. 5. When therefore they see those, over
whom they are now exalted, (but) who shall then be
exalted and glorified more than they, they shall
respectively be transformed, the latter into the
splendour of angels, and the former shall yet more
waste away in wonder at the visions and in the
beholding of the forms. 6. For they will first behold,
and afterwards depart to be tormented.

7. But those who have been saved by their works,
And to whom the Law hath been now a hope,
And understanding an expectation,
And wisdom a confidence,
To them wonders will appear in their time.

8. For they shall behold the world which is now
invisible to them,
And they shall behold the time which is now
hidden from them.

9. And time shall no longer age them.

10. For in the heights of that world shall they dwell,
And they shall be made like unto the angels,
And be made equal to the stars,
And they shall be changed into every form they
desire,
From beauty into loveliness,
And from light into the splendour of glory.

11. For there shall be spread before them the

extents of Paradise, and there shall be shown to them the beauty of the majesty of the living creatures which are beneath the throne, and all the armies of the angels, who [are now held fast by My word, lest they should appear, and] are held fast by a command, that they may stand in their places till their advent cometh. 12. Moreover, there shall then be excellency in the righteous surpassing that in the angels. 13. For the first shall receive the last, those whom they were expecting, and the last those of whom they used to hear that they had passed away.

14. For they have been delivered from this world of tribulation,
    And laid down the burthen of anguish.

15. For what then have men lost their life,
    And for what have those who were on the earth exchanged their soul?

16. For then they chose (not) for themselves this time,
    Which, beyond the reach of anguish, could not pass away;
    But they chose for themselves that time,
    Whose issues are full of lamentations and evils,
    And they denied the world which ageth not those who come to it,
    And they have rejected the time of glory,
    So that they shall not come to the honour of which I told thee before."

LII. And I answered and said:
    " How can **we** forget those for whom woe is then reserved?

2. And why therefore again do we mourn for those who die?
    Or why do we weep for those who depart to Sheol?

3. Let lamentations be reserved for the beginning of that coming torment,
    And let tears be laid up for the advent of the destruction of that time.

4. [But even in the face of these things I will speak.

5. And as for the righteous, what will they do now?

6. Rejoice ye in the suffering which ye now suffer :
For why do ye look for the decline of your
enemies? 7. Make ready your soul for that
which is reserved for you,
And prepare your souls for the reward which
is laid up for you."]

LIII.–LXXIV. **The Messiah Apocalypse.**

LIII. *The Vision of the Cloud and the Waters.*

LIII. And when I had said these things I fell
asleep there, and I saw a vision, and lo ! a cloud was
ascending from a very great sea, and I kept gazing
upon it, and lo ! it was full of waters white and black,
and there were many colours in those self-same
waters, and as it were the likeness of great lightning
was seen at its summit. 2. And I saw that cloud
passing swiftly in quick courses, and it covered all
the earth. 3. And it came to pass after these things
that that cloud began to pour upon the earth the
waters that were in it. 4. And I saw that there was
not one and the same likeness in the waters which
descended from it. 5. For in the first beginning they
were black **and many** for a time, and afterwards I
saw that the waters became bright, but they were
not many, and after these things again I saw black
(waters), and after these things again bright, and
again black and again bright. 6. Now this was done
twelve times, but the black were always more numerous than the bright. 7. And it came to pass at the
end of the cloud, that lo ! it rained black waters, and
they were darker than had been all those waters
that were before, and fire was mingled with them,
and where those waters descended, they wrought
devastation and destruction. 8. And I saw after
these things that lightning which I had seen on the
summit of the cloud, that it seized hold of it and
hurled it to the earth. 9. Now that lightning shone
exceedingly, so as to illuminate the whole earth, and
it healed those regions where the last waters had
descended and wrought devastation. 10. And it

took hold of the whole earth and had dominion over
it.   11. And I saw after these things, and lo ! twelve
rivers were ascending from the sea, and they began
to surround that lightning and to become subject
to it   12. And by reason of my fear I awoke.

LIV.–LV. Baruch's Prayer.

LIV. And I besought the Mighty One, and said :
  " Thou alone, O Lord, knowest of aforetime the
    deep things of the world,
  And the things which befall in their times Thou
    bringest about by Thy word,
  And against the works of the inhabitants of
    the earth Thou dost hasten the beginnings
    of the times,
  And the end of the seasons Thou alone knowest.
2. For Whom nothing is too hard,
  But Thou doest everything easily by a nod.
3. To whom the depths as the heights are accessible.
  And the beginnings of the ages minister to Thy
    word.
4. Who revealest to those who fear **Thee** what is
    prepared for them,
  That henceforth they may be comforted.
5. Thou showest great acts to those who know not ;
  Thou breakest up the enclosure of those who
    are ignorant,
  And lightest up what is dark,
  And revealest what is hidden to the pure,
  [Who in faith have submitted themselves to
    Thee and Thy Law.]
6. Thou hast shown to Thy servant this vision ;
  Reveal to me also its interpretation.
7. For I know that as regards those things wherein
I besought Thee, I have received a response, and as
regards what I besought, Thou didst reveal to me,
and didst show me with what voice I should praise
Thee, or from what members I should cause praises
and hallelujahs to ascend to Thee.
8. For if my members were mouths,

And the hairs of my head voices,
Even so I could not give Thee the meed of praise,
Nor laud Thee as is befitting,
Nor could I recount Thy praise,
Nor tell the glory of Thy beauty.

9. For what am I amongst men,
Or why am I reckoned amongst those who are
more excellent than I,
That I should have heard all those marvellous
things from the Most High,
And promises numberless from Him Who
created me?

10. Blessed be my mother amongst those that bear,
And praised among women be she that bare me.

11. For I will not be silent in praising the Mighty
One,
And with the voice of praise I will recount His
marvellous deeds.

12. For who doeth like unto Thy marvellous deeds,
O God,
Or who comprehendeth Thy deep thought of life?

13. For with Thy counsel dost Thou govern all the
creatures which Thy right hand hath created,
And Thou hast established every fountain of
light beside Thee,
And the treasures of wisdom beneath Thy
throne hast Thou prepared.

14. And justly do they perish who have not loved
Thy Law,
And the torment of judgement shall await
those who have not submitted themselves to
Thy power.

15. For though Adam first sinned,
And brought untimely death upon all,
Yet of those who were born from him
Each one of them hath prepared for his own
soul torment to come,
And, again, each one of them hath chosen for
himself glories to come.

[16. For assuredly he who believeth shall receive
reward.

17. But now, as for you, ye wicked that now are,
     turn ye to destruction, because ye will speedily
     be visited, in that formerly ye rejected the
     understanding of the Most High.

18. For His works have not taught you,
     Nor hath the skill of His creation, which is at
     all times, persuaded you.]

19. Adam is therefore not the cause, save only of
     his own soul,
     But each one of us hath been the Adam of his
     own soul.

20. But do Thou, O Lord, expound to me regarding
     those things which Thou hast revealed to me,
     And inform me regarding that which I besought
     Thee.

21. For at the consummation of the world there
     shall be vengeance taken upon those who
     have done wickedness according to their
     wickedness;
     And Thou wilt glorify the faithful according to
     their faithfulness.

22. For those who are amongst Thine own Thou
     rulest,
     And those who sin Thou blottest out from
     amongst Thine own."

LV. And it came to pass when I had finished
speaking the words of this prayer, that I sat there
under a tree, that I might rest in the shade of the
branches. 2. And I wondered and was astonied,
and pondered in my thoughts regarding the multitude of goodness which sinners who are upon the
earth have rejected, and regarding the great torment
which they have despised, though they knew that
they should be tormented because of the sin they had
committed. 3. And when I was pondering on these
things and the like, lo ! the angel Ramiel, who pre-
sideth over true visions, was sent to me, and he said
unto me : 4. " Why doth thy heart trouble thee,
Baruch, and why doth thy thought disturb thee ?

5. For if **owing** to the report **which** thou hast
only heard of judgement thou art so moved, what

(wilt thou be) when thou shalt see it manifestly with thine eyes? 6. And if with the expectation wherewith thou dost expect the day of the Mighty One thou art so overcome, what (wilt thou be) when thou shalt come to its advent? 7. And, if at the word of the announcement of the torment of those who have done foolishly thou art so wholly distraught, how much more when the event will reveal marvellous things? 8. And if thou hast heard tidings of the good and evil things which are then coming, and art grieved, what (wilt thou be) when thou shalt behold what the majesty will reveal, which will convict these and cause those to rejoice?"

LVI.–LXXIV. The Interpretation of the Vision.

LVI. "Nevertheless, because thou hast besought the Most High to reveal to thee the interpretation of the vision which thou hast seen, I have been sent to tell thee. 2. And the Mighty One hath assuredly made known to thee the methods of the times that have passed, and of those that are destined to pass in His world from the beginning of its creations even unto its consummation, of those things which (are) deceit and of those which (are) in truth. 3. For as thou didst see a great cloud which ascended from the sea, and went and covered the earth, this is the duration of the world (= αἰών) which the Mighty One made when He took counsel to make the world. 4. And it came to pass when the word had gone forth from His presence, that the duration of the world had come into being in a small degree, and **was established** according to the multitude of the intelligence of Him Who sent it. 5. And as thou didst previously see on the summit of the cloud black waters which descended previously on the earth, this is the transgression wherewith Adam the first man transgressed.

  6. For since when he transgressed
      Untimely death came into being,
      And grief was named, and anguish was prepared,

And pain was created,
And trouble consummated,
And disease began to be established,
And Sheol to demand that it should be renewed
in blood,
And the begetting of children was brought about,
And the passion of parents produced,
And the greatness of humanity was humiliated,
And goodness languished.

7. What therefore can be blacker or darker than these things? 8. This is the beginning of the black waters which thou hast seen. 9. And from these black (waters) again were black derived, and the darkness of darkness produced 10. For he became a danger to his own soul, even to the angels became he a danger. 11. For, moreover, at that time when he was created, they enjoyed liberty. 12. And some of them descended, and mingled with women. 13. And then those who did so were tormented in chains. 14. But the rest of the multitude of the angels, of which there is ⟨no⟩ number, restrained themselves. 15. And those who dwelt on the earth perished together (with them) through the waters of the deluge. 16. These are the black first waters.

LVII. And after these (waters) thou didst see bright waters : this is the fount of Abraham, also his generations and advent of his son, and of his son's son, and of those like them. 2. Because at that time the unwritten Law was named amongst them,

And the works of the commandments were then
fulfilled,
And belief in the coming judgement was then
generated,
And hope of the world that was to be renewed
was then built up,
And the promise of the life that should come
hereafter was implanted.

3. These are the bright waters, which thou hast seen.

LVIII. And the black third waters which thou hast seen, these are the mingling of all sins, which the nations afterwards wrought after the death of those righteous men, and the wickedness of the land of Egypt, wherein they did wickedly in the service wherewith they made their sons to serve. 2. Nevertheless, these also perished at last.

LIX. And the bright fourth waters which thou hast seen are the advent of Moses and Aaron and Miriam and Joshua the son of Nun and Caleb and of all those like them. 2. For at that time the lamp of the eternal Law shone on all those who sat in darkness, which announced to them that believe the promise of their reward, and to them that deny, the torment of fire which is reserved for them. 3. But also the heavens at that time were shaken from their place, and those who were under the throne of the Mighty One were perturbed, when He was taking Moses unto Himself. 4. For He showed him many admonitions together with the principles of the **Law** and the consummation of **times,** as also to thee, and likewise the pattern of Zion and its measures, **in the pattern of which the sanctuary** of the present time was to be made. 5. But then also He showed to him the measures of the fire, also the depths of the abyss and the weight of the winds and the number of the drops of rain. 6. And the suppression of anger, and the multitude of long-suffering, and the truth of judgement. 7. And the root of wisdom, and the riches of understanding, and the fount of knowledge; 8. And the height of the air, and the greatness of Paradise, and the consummation of the ages, and the beginning of the day of judgement; 9. And the number of the offerings, and the earths which have not yet come. 10. And the mouth of Gehenna, and the station of vengeance, and the place of faith, and the region of hope; 11. And the likeness of future torment, and the multitude of innumerable angels, and the flaming hosts, and the splendour of the lightnings, and the voice of the thunders, and the orders of the **chiefs** of the angels, and the treasuries of light, and the changes of the times, and the investigations of the Law. 12. These are the bright fourth waters which thou hast seen.

LX. And the black fifth waters which thou hast seen raining are the works which the Amorites wrought, and the spells of their incantations which they wrought, and the wickedness of their mysteries, and the mingling of their pollution. 2. But even Israel was then polluted by sins in the days of the **Judges,** though they saw many signs which were from Him Who made them.

LXI. And the bright sixth waters which thou didst see, this is the time in which David and Solomon were born.

2. And there was at that time the building of Zion,
   And the dedication of the sanctuary,
   And the shedding of much blood of the nations that sinned then,
   And many offerings which were offered then in the dedication of the sanctuary.
3. And peace and tranquillity existed at that time.
4. And wisdom was heard in the assembly,
   And the riches of understanding were magnified in the congregations,
5. And the holy festivals were fulfilled in goodness and in much joy,
6. And the judgement of the rulers was then seen to be without guile,
   And the righteousness of the precepts of the Mighty One was accomplished with truth,
7. And the land [which] was then beloved **by the Lord,**
   And because its inhabitants sinned not, it was glorified beyond all lands,
   And the city of Zion ruled then over all lands and regions.
8. These are the bright waters which thou hast seen.

LXII. And the black seventh waters which thou hast seen, this is the perversion (brought about) by the counsel of Jeroboam, who took counsel to make two calves of gold. 2. And all the iniquities which the kings who were after him iniquitously wrought. 3. And the curse of Jezebel, and the worship of idols which Israel practised at that time. 4. And the withholding of rain, and the famines which occurred until women ate the fruit of their wombs. 5. And the time of their captivity which came upon the nine tribes and a half, because they were in many sins. 6. And Salmanasar king of Assyria came and led them away captive. 7. But regarding the Gentiles it were tedious to tell how they always wrought impiety and wickedness, and never wrought righteousness. 8. These are the black seventh waters which thou hast seen.

LXIII. And the bright eighth waters which thou hast seen, this is the rectitude and uprightness of Hezekiah king of Judah and the **grace** ⟨of God⟩ which came upon him. 2. For when Sennacherib was stirred up in order that he might perish, and his wrath troubled him in order that he might thereby perish, for the multitude also of the nations which were with him. 3. When, moreover, Hezekiah the king heard those things which the king of Assyria was devising (*i. e.*) to come and seize him and destroy his people, the two and a half tribes which remained; nay, more, he wished to overthrow Zion also; then Hezekiah trusted in his works, and had hope in his righteousness, and spake with the Mighty One and said : 4. ' Behold, for lo ! Sennacherib is prepared to destroy us, and he will be boastful and uplifted when he hath destroyed Zion.'

5. And the Mighty One heard him, for Hezekiah was wise,

And He had respect unto his prayer, because he was righteous.

6. And thereupon the Mighty One commanded Ramiel His angel who speaketh with thee. 7. And I went forth and destroyed their multitude, the number of whose chiefs only was a hundred and eighty-five thousand, and each one of them had an equal number (at his command). 8. And at that time I burned their bodies within, but their raiment and arms I preserved outwardly, in order that the still more wonderful deeds of the Mighty One might appear, and that thereby His name might be spoken

of throughout the whole earth. 9. Moreover, Zion was saved and Jerusalem delivered; Israel also was freed from tribulation. 10. And all those who were in the holy land rejoiced, and the name of the Mighty One was glorified so that it was spoken of. 11. These are the bright waters which thou hast seen.

LXIV. And the black ninth waters which thou hast seen, this is all the wickedness which was in the days of Manasseh, the son of Hezekiah. 2. For he wrought much impiety, and he slew the righteous, and he wrested judgement, and he shed the blood of the innocent, and wedded women he violently polluted, and he overturned the altars, and destroyed their offerings, and drave forth the priests lest they should minister in the sanctuary. 3. And he made an image with five faces; four of them looked to the four winds, and the fifth on the summit of the image as an adversary of the zeal of the Mighty One. 4. And then wrath went forth from the presence of the Mighty One to the intent that Zion should be rooted out, as also it befell in your days. 5. But also against the two tribes and a half went forth a decree that they should also be led away captive, as thou hast now seen. 6. And to such a degree did the impiety of Manasseh increase, that it removed the praise of the Most High from the sanctuary. 7. On this account Manasseh was at that time named 'the impious,' and finally his abode was in the fire. 8. For though his prayer was heard with the Most High, finally, when he was cast into the brazen horse and the brazen horse was melted, it served as a sign unto him at the time. 9. For he did not live perfectly, for he was not worthy—but that thenceforward he might know by whom finally he should be tormented. 10. For he who is able to benefit is also able to torment.

LXV. Thus, moreover, did Manasseh act impiously, and thought that in his time the Mighty One would not inquire into these things. 2. These are the black ninth waters which thou hast seen.

LXVI. And the bright tenth waters which thou hast seen : this is the purity of the generations of

Josiah king of Judah, who was the only one at that time who submitted himself to the Mighty One with all his heart and with all his soul. 2. And he cleansed the land from idols, and hallowed all the vessels which had been polluted, and restored the offerings to the altar, and raised the horn of the holy, and exalted the righteous, and glorified all that were wise in understanding, and brought back the priests to their ministry, and destroyed and removed the magicians and enchanters and necromancers from the land. 3. And not only did he slay the impious that were living, but they also took from the sepulchres the bones of the dead and burned them with fire. 4. [And the festivals and the sabbaths he established in their sanctity], and their polluted ones he burnt in the fire, and the lying prophets which deceived the people, these also he burnt in the fire, and the people who listened to them when they were living, he cast them into the brook Cedron, and heaped stones upon them. 5. And he was zealous with the zeal of the Mighty One with all his soul, and he alone was firm in the Law at that time, so that he left none that was uncircumcised, or that wrought impiety in all the land, all the days of his life. 6. **Therefore** he shall receive an eternal reward, and he shall be glorified with the Mighty One beyond many at a later time. 7. For on his account and on account of those who are like him were the honourable glories, of which thou wast told before, created and prepared. 8. These are the bright waters which thou hast seen.

LXVII. And the black eleventh waters which thou hast seen : this is the calamity which is now befalling Zion.

2. Dost thou think that there is no anguish to the angels in the presence of the Mighty One,

That Zion was so delivered up,

And that lo ! the Gentiles boast in their hearts,

And **assemble** before their idols and say :

' She is trodden down who ofttimes trod down,

And she hath been reduced to servitude who reduced (others) ? '

3. Dost thou think that in these things the Most
   High rejoiceth,
   Or that His name is glorified?
4. [But how will it serve towards His righteous
   judgement?]
5. Yet after these things shall the dispersed among
   the Gentiles be taken hold of by tribulation,
   And in shame shall they dwell in every place.
6. Because so far as Zion is delivered up,
   And Jerusalem laid waste,
   And idols prosper in the cities of the Gentiles,
   And the vapour of the smoke of the incense of
   righteousness which is by the Law is extin-
   guished in Zion,
   And in the region of Zion, in every place, lo !
   there is the smoke of impiety.
7. But the king of Babylon will arise who hath
   now destroyed Zion,
   And he will boast over the people,
   And he will speak great things in his heart in
   the presence of the Most High.
8. But he also shall fall at last.
9. These are the black waters.

LXVIII. And the bright twelfth waters which
thou hast seen : this is the word. 2. For after these
things a time shall come when thy people shall fall
into distress, so that they shall all run the risk of
perishing together. 3. Nevertheless, they shall be
saved, and their enemies shall fall in their presence.
4. And they shall have in (due) time much joy.
5. And at that time after a little interval Zion shall
again be builded, and its offerings shall again be
restored, and the priests shall return to their ministry,
and again the Gentiles shall come to glorify it.
6. Nevertheless, not fully as in the beginning. 7. But
it shall come to pass after these things that there
shall be the fall of many nations. 8. These are the
bright waters which thou hast seen.

LXIX. For the last waters which thou hast seen
which were darker than all that were before them,
those which were after the twelfth number, which

F

were collected together, belong to the whole world.
2. For the Most High made division from the beginning because He alone knoweth what shall befall.
3. For as to the enormities **and** the impieties which should be wrought before Him, He foresaw six kinds of them. 4. And of the good works of the righteous which should be accomplished before Him, He foresaw six kinds of them, beyond those which He should work at the consummation of the age. 5. On this account there were not black waters with black, nor bright with bright; for it is the consummation.

LXX. Hear therefore the interpretation of the last black waters which are to come [after the black]: this is the word: 2. Behold! the days come, and it shall be when the time of the age has ripened,

And the harvest of its evil and good seeds hath come,

That the Mighty One will bring upon the earth and its inhabitants and upon its rulers

Perturbation of **spirit** and stupor of heart.

3. And they will hate one another,
And provoke one another to fight,
And the mean shall rule over the honourable,
And those of low degree shall be extolled above the famous,

4. And the many shall be delivered into the hands of the few,
And those who are nothing shall rule over the strong,
And the poor shall have abundance beyond the rich,
And the impious shall exalt themselves above the heroic,

5. And the wise shall be silent,
And the foolish shall speak,
Neither shall the thought of men be then confirmed,
Nor the counsel of the **mighty,**
Nor shall the hope of those who hope be confirmed;

6. Moreover, it shall be when those things which
were predicted have come to pass,
That confusion shall fall upon all men,
And some of them shall fall in battle,
And some of them shall perish in anguish,
And some of them shall be **destroyed** by their
own.

7. Then the Most High will reveal those peoples
whom He hath prepared before,
And they shall come and make war with the
leaders that shall then be left.

8. And it shall come to pass that whosoever
getteth safe out of the war shall die in the earth-
quake, and whosoever getteth safe out of the earth-
quake shall be burned by the fire, and whosoever
getteth safe out of the fire **shall be destroyed** by
famine. [9. And it shall come to pass that whosoever of the victors and the vanquished getteth
safe out of and escapeth all these things aforesaid
shall be delivered into the hands of My servant
Messiah.] 10. For all the earth will devour its
inhabitants.

LXXI. And the holy land shall have mercy on
its own,
And it shall protect its nhabiters at that time.

2. This is the vision which thou hast seen, and
this is the interpretation. 3. For I have come to
tell thee these things, because thy prayer hath been
heard with the Most High.

LXXII. Hear now also regarding the bright **lightning** which is to come at the consummation after
these black (waters), this is the word : 2. After the
signs have come, of which thou wast told before,
when the nations become turbulent, and the time of
My Messiah is come, He shall both summon all the
nations, and some of them He shall spare, and some
of them He shall slay. 3. These things therefore
shall come upon the nations which are to be spared
by Him. 4. Every nation which knoweth not Israel,
and hath not trodden down the seed of Jacob, shall

indeed be spared.   5. And this because some of every nation shall be subjected to thy people.   6. But all those who have ruled over you, or have known you, shall be given up to the sword.

LXXIII. And it shall come to pass, when He hath brought low everything that is in the world,

And hath sat down in peace for the age on the throne of His kingdom,

That joy shall then be revealed,

And rest appear;

2. And then healing shall descend in dew,

And disease shall withdraw,

And anxiety and anguish and lamentation shall pass from amongst men,

And gladness shall proceed through the whole earth;

3. And no one shall again die untimely,

Nor shall any adversity suddenly befall,

4. And judgements, and revilings, and contentions, and revenges,

And blood, and passions, and envy, and hatred,

And whatsoever things are like these shall go into condemnation when they are removed.

5. For it is these very things which have filled this world with evils,

And on account of these the life of man has been greatly troubled.

6. And wild beasts shall come from the forest and minister unto men,

And asps and dragons shall come forth from their holes to submit themselves to a little child,

7. And women shall no longer then have pain when they bear,

Nor shall they suffer torment when they yield the fruit of the womb.

LXXIV. And it shall come to pass in those days that the reapers shall not grow weary,

Nor those that build be toilworn;

For the works shall of themselves speedily advance

With those who do them in much tranquillity.

2. For that time is the consummation of that
which is corruptible,
And the beginning of that which is not corruptible.

3. Therefore those things which were predicted
shall belong to it;
Therefore it is far away from evils, and near to
those things which die not.

4. This is the bright lightning which came after
the last dark waters.''

LXXV. **Baruch's Hymn.**

LXXV. And I answered and said :
" Who can **understand,** O Lord, Thy goodness?
For it is incomprehensible.

2. Or who can search into Thy compassions,
Which are infinite?

3. Or who can comprehend Thy intelligence?

4. Or who is able to recount the thoughts of Thy
mind?

5. Or who of those that are born can hope to
come to those things,
Unless he is one to whom Thou art merciful
and gracious?

6. Because, if assuredly Thou didst not have
compassion on man,
Those who are under Thy right hand,
They could not come to those things,
But those who are in the numbers named can
be called.

7. But if, indeed, we who exist know wherefore we
have come,
And submit ourselves to Him Who brought us
out of Egypt,
We shall come again and remember those things
which have passed,
And shall rejoice regarding that which hath
been.

8. But if now we know not wherefore we have come,

And recognise not the principate of Him Who
   brought us up out of Egypt,
We shall come again and seek after those things
   which have been now,
And be grieved with pain because of those things
   which have befallen."

LXXVI. **Baruch is bidden to instruct the People.**

LXXVI. And He answered and said unto me :
[" Inasmuch as the revelation of this vision hath
been interpreted to thee as thou besoughtest], hear
the word of the Most High that thou mayest know
what is to befall thee after these things. 2. For
thou shalt surely depart from this earth, nevertheless
not unto death; but **thou shalt be preserved unto
the consummation** of the times. 3. Go up, therefore,
to the top of that mountain, and there shall pass
before thee all the regions of that land, and the
figure of the inhabited world, and the tops of the
mountains, and the depths of the valleys, and
the depths of the seas, and the number of the rivers,
that thou mayest see what thou art leaving, and
whither thou art going. 4. Now this shall befall
after forty days. 5. Go now, therefore, during these
days and instruct the people so far as thou art able,
that they may learn so as not to die at the last
times, but may learn in order that they may live at
the last times."

LXXVII. 1–16. **Baruch's Admonition to the People.**

LXXVII. And I, Baruch, went thence and came
to the people, and assembled them together from the
greatest to the least, and said unto them : 2. " Hear,
ye children of Israel, behold how many ye are who
remain of the twelve tribes of Israel. 3. For to you
and to your fathers the Lord gave a Law more

excellent than to all peoples.   4. And because your brethren transgressed the commandments of the Most High,

> He brought vengeance upon you and upon them,
> And He spared not the former,
> And the latter also He gave into captivity,
> And left not a residue of them.

5. And behold ! ye are here with me ;
6. If, therefore, ye direct your ways aright,
> You also shall not depart as your brethren departed,
> But they shall come to you.

7. For He is merciful Whom ye worship,
> And He is gracious in Whom ye hope,
> And He is true, so that He shall do (you) good and not evil.

8. Have ye not seen here what hath befallen Zion ?
9. Or do ye, perchance, think that the place had sinned,
> And that on this account it was overthrown ?
> Or that the land had wrought foolishness,
> And that therefore it was delivered up?

10. And know ye not that on account of you who did sin,
> That which sinned not was overthrown,
> And, on account of those who wrought wickedly,
> That which wrought not foolishness was delivered up to (its) enemies? "

11. And the whole people answered and said unto me : " So far as we can recall the good things which the Mighty One hath done unto us, we do recall them ; and those things which we do not remember He in His mercy knoweth. 12. Nevertheless, do this for us thy people : write also to our brethren in Babylon an epistle of doctrine and a scroll of hope, that thou mayest confirm them also before thou dost depart from us.

13. For the shepherds of Israel have perished,
> And the lamps which gave light are extinguished,

And the fountains have withheld their stream
whence we used to drink.
14. And we are left in the darkness,
And amid the trees of the forest,
And the thirst of the wilderness."
15. And I answered and said unto them :
" Shepherds and lamps and fountains came from
the Law ;
And though we depart, yet the Law abideth.
16. If, therefore, ye have respect to the Law,
And are intent upon wisdom,
A lamp shall not be wanting,
And a **shepherd** shall not fail,
And a fountain shall not dry up.

LXXVII. 17–26. **The Sending of the Epistles.**

17. Nevertheless, as ye said unto me, I will write
also unto your brethren in Babylon, and I will send
by means of men, and I will write in like manner to
the nine tribes and a half, and send by means of a
bird."   18. And it came to pass on the one and
twentieth day in the eighth month that I, Baruch,
came and sat down under the oak, under the shadow
of the branches, and no man was with me, but I was
alone.   19. And I wrote these two epistles : one I
sent by an eagle to the nine and a half tribes ; and
the other I sent to those that were at Babylon, by
means of three men.   20. And I called the eagle,
and spake these words unto it :   21. " The Most
High hath made thee that thou shouldst be higher
than all birds.   22. And now go, and tarry not in
(any) place, nor enter a nest, nor settle upon any
tree, till thou hast passed over the breadth of the
many waters of the river Euphrates, and hast gone
to the people that dwell there, and cast down to
them this epistle.   23. Remember, moreover, that,
at the time of the deluge, Noah received from the
dove the fruit of the olive, when he sent it forth
from the ark.   24. Yea, also the ravens ministered
to Elijah, bearing him food, as they had been com-

manded.   25. Solomon also, in the time of his kingdom, whithersoever he wished to send or seek for
anything, commanded a bird (to go thither), and it
obeyed him as he commanded it.   26. And now let
it not weary thee, and turn not to the right hand
nor to the left, but fly and go by a direct way, that
thou mayest preserve the command of the Mighty
One, according as I said unto thee."

LXXVIII.–LXXXVI. The Epistle of Baruch, the Son of Neriah, which he wrote to the nine and a half Tribes.

LXXVIII. These are the words of that epistle
which Baruch, the son of Neriah, sent to the nine and
a half tribes, which were across the river Euphrates,
in which these things were written.   2. Thus saith
Baruch, the son of Neriah, to the brethren carried
into captivity : "Mercy and peace.   3. I bear in
mind, my brethren, the love of Him Who created
us, Who loved us from of old, and never hated us,
but above all educated us.   4. And truly I know
that, behold, all we the twelve tribes are bound by
one bond, inasmuch as we are born from one father.
5. Wherefore I have been the more careful to leave
you the words of this epistle before I die, that ye
may be comforted regarding the evils which have
come upon you, and that ye may be grieved also
regarding the evil that hath befallen your brethren;
and again, also, that ye may justify His judgement
which He hath decreed against you that ye should
be carried away captive—for what ye have suffered
is disproportioned to what ye have done—in order
that, at the last times, ye may be found worthy of
your fathers.   6. Therefore, if ye consider that ye
have now suffered those things for your good, that
ye may not finally be condemned and tormented,
then ye shall receive eternal hope; if, above all, ye
destroy from your heart vain error, on account of
which ye departed hence.   7. For if ye so do these
things, He will continually remember you, He Who

always promised on our behalf to those who were more excellent than we, that He will never forget nor forsake us, but with much mercy will gather together again those who were dispersed.

LXXIX. Now, my brethren, learn first what befell Zion : how that Nebuchadnezzar, king of Babylon, came up against us. 2. For we have sinned against Him Who made us, and we have not kept the commandments which He commanded us, yet He hath not chastened us as we deserved. 3. For what befell you we also suffer in a pre-eminent degree, for it befell us also.

LXXX. And now, my brethren, I make known unto you that when the enemy had surrounded the city, the angels of the Most High were sent, and they overthrew the fortifications of the strong wall, and they destroyed the firm iron corners, which could not be rooted out. 2. Nevertheless, they hid **all** the vessels of the sanctuary, lest **the enemy should get possession of them.** 3. And when they had done these things, they delivered thereupon to the enemy the overthrown wall, and the plundered house, and the burnt temple, and the people who were overcome because they were delivered up, lest the enemy should boast and say : ' Thus by force have we been able to lay waste even the house of the Most High in war.' 4. Your brethren also they have bound and led away to Babylon, and have caused them to dwell there. 5. But we have been left here, being very few. 6. This is the tribulation about which I wrote to you. 7. For assuredly I know that ⟨the consolation of⟩ the inhabitants of Zion consoleth you ; so far as ye knew that it was prospered (your consolation) was greater than the tribulation which ye endured in having departed from it.

LXXXI. But regarding consolation, hear ye the word. 2. For I was mourning regarding Zion, and I prayed for mercy from the Most High, and I said : 3. ' How long will these things endure for us ? And will these evils come upon us always ? '

4. And the Mighty One did according to the
   multitude of His mercies,
   And the Most High according to the greatness
   of His compassion.
   And He revealed unto me the word that I
   might receive consolation.
   And He showed me visions that I should not
   again endure anguish.
   And He made known to me the mystery of the
   times,
   And the advent of the hours He showed me.

LXXXII. Therefore, my brethren, I have written
to you, that ye may comfort yourselves regarding
the multitude of your tribulations. 2. For know ye
that our Maker will assuredly avenge us on all our
enemies, according to all that they have done to us,
also that the consummation which the Most High
will make is very high, and His mercy that is coming,
and the consummation of His judgement, is by no
means far off.

3. For lo ! we see now the multitude of the pros-
   perity of the Gentiles,
   Though they act impiously,
   But they shall be like a vapour.

4. And we behold the multitude of their power,
   Though they do wickedly,
   But they shall be made like unto a drop.

5. And we see the firmness of their might,
   Though they resist the Mighty One every hour,
   But they shall be accounted as spittle.

6. And we consider the glory of their greatness,
   Though they do not keep the statutes of the
   Most High,
   But as smoke shall they pass away.

7. And we meditate on the beauty of their grace-
   fulness,
   Though they have to do with pollutions,
   But as grass that withers shall they fade away.

8. And we consider the strength of their cruelty,
   Though they remember not the end (thereof),
   But as a wave that passeth shall they be broken.

9. And we remark the boastfulness of their might,
> Though they deny the beneficence of God, Who gave (it) to them,

But they shall pass away as a passing cloud.

LXXXIII. [For the Most High shall assuredly hasten His times,
> And He shall assuredly bring on His hours.

2. And He shall assuredly judge those who are in His world,
> And shall visit in truth all things by means of all their hidden works.

3. And He shall assuredly examine the secret thoughts,
> And that which is laid up in the secret chambers of all the members of man,
> And shall make (them) manifest in the presence of all with reproof.

4. Let none, therefore, of these present things ascend into your hearts; but, above all, let us be expectant, because that which is promised to us shall come. 5. And let us not now look unto the delights of the Gentiles in the present, but let us remember what hath been promised to us in the end. 6. For the ends of the times and of the seasons and whatsoever is with them shall assuredly pass by together. 7. The consummation, moreover, of the age shall then show the great might of its ruler, when all things come to judgement. 8. Do ye, therefore, prepare your hearts for that which before ye believed, lest ye come to be in bondage in both worlds, so that ye be led away captive here and be tormented there. 9. For (as to) that which existeth now, or which hath passed away, or which is to come, in all these things, neither is the evil fully evil, nor, again, the good fully good.

10. For all healthinesses of this time are turning into diseases,

11. And all might of this time is turning into weakness,
> And all the force of this time is turning into impotence,

12. And every energy of youth is turning into old age and consummation,
    And every beauty of gracefulness of this time is turning faded and hateful,
13. And every proud dominion of the present is turning into humiliation and shame,
14. And every praise of the glory of this time is turning into the shame of silence,
    And every vain splendour and insolence of this time is turning into voiceless ruin,
15. And every delight and joy of this time is turning to worms and corruption,
16. And every clamour of the pride of this time is turning into dust and stillness,
17. And every possession of riches of this time is being turned into Sheol alone,
18. And all the rapine of passion of this time is turning into involuntary death,
    And every passion of the lusts of this time is turning into a judgement of torment;
19. And every artifice and craftiness of this time is turning into a proof of the truth,
20. And every sweetness of unguents of this time is turning into judgement and condemnation,
21. And every love of lying is turning to contumely through truth.
22. Since, therefore, all these things are done now, doth any one think that they will not be avenged?
23. But the consummation of all things shall come to the truth.]

LXXXIV. Behold! I have therefore made known unto you (these things) whilst I live; for I said that ye should learn the things that are excellent; for the Mighty One hath commanded to instruct you; and I will set before you some of the commandments of His judgement before I die. 2. Remember that formerly Moses assuredly called heaven and earth to witness against you, and said : ' If ye transgress the Law ye shall be dispersed, but if ye keep it ye shall be kept.' 3. And other things also he used to say unto you when ye, the twelve tribes. were together in the desert. 4. And after his death ye cast them away from you; on this account there came upon you what had been predicted. 5. And now Moses used to tell you before they befell you, and lo! they have befallen you; for you have forsaken the Law. 6. Lo! I also say unto you after ye have suffered, that if ye obey those things which have been said unto you, ye shall receive from the Mighty One whatever hath been laid up and reserved for you. 7. Moreover, let this epistle be for a testimony between me and you, that ye may remember the commandments of the Mighty One, and that also there may be to me a defence in the presence of Him Who sent me. 8. And remember ye the Law and Zion, and the holy land and your brethren, and the covenant of your fathers, and forget not the festivals and the sabbaths. 9. And deliver ye this epistle and the traditions of the Law to your sons after you, as also your fathers delivered (them) to you. 10. And at all times make request persever-ingly and pray diligently with your whole heart that the Mighty One may be reconciled to you, and that He may not reckon the multitude of your sins, but remember the rectitude of your fathers. 11. For if He judge us not according to the multitude of His mercies, woe unto all us who are born.

LXXXV. [Know ye, moreover, that

In former times and in the generations of old
those our fathers had helpers,
Righteous men and holy prophets;

2. Nay, more, we were in our own land,
And they helped us when we sinned
And they interceded for us to Him Who made
us,
Because they trusted in their works,
And the Mighty One heard their prayer and
forgave us.

3. But now the righteous have been gathered,
And the prophets have fallen asleep,
And we also have gone forth from the land,
And Zion hath been taken from us;

And we have nothing now save the Mighty One
and His Law.

4. If, therefore, we direct and dispose our hearts,
We shall receive everything that we lost,
And much better things than we lost by many
times.

5. For what we have lost was subject to corruption,
And what we shall receive shall not be corruptible.

6. Moreover, also, I have written thus to our
brethren to Babylon, that to them also I may
attest these very things.

7. And let all those things aforesaid be always
before your eyes,
Because we are still in the spirit and the power
of our liberty.

8. Again, moreover, the Most High also is long-
suffering towards us here,
And He hath shown to us that which is to be,
And hath not concealed from us what shall befall
in the end.

9. Before, therefore, judgement exact its own,
And truth that which is its due,
Let us prepare our soul,
That we may enter into possession of, and not
be taken possession of,
And that we may hope and not be put to shame,
And that we may rest with our fathers, and not
be tormented with our enemies.

10. For the youth of the world is past,
And the strength of the creation is already
exhausted,
And the advent of the times is very short,
Yea, they have passed by;
And the pitcher is near to the cistern,
And the ship to the port,
And the course of the journey to the city,
And life to (its) consummation.

11. And, again, prepare your souls, so that when
ye sail and ascend from the ship ye may have rest,
and not be condemned when ye depart.   12. For lo !
when the Most High shall bring to pass all these things,

There shall not be there again a place of repent-
 ance, nor a limit to the times,
Nor a duration for the hours,
Nor a change of ways,
Nor place for prayer
Nor sending of petitions,
Nor receiving of knowledge,
Nor giving of love,
Nor place of repentance for the soul,
Nor supplication for offences,
Nor intercession of the fathers,
Nor prayer of the prophets,
Nor help of the righteous.

13. There there is the sentence of corruption,
 The way of fire,
 And the path which bringeth to Gehenna.

14. On this account there is one Law by One,
 One age and an end for all who are in it.

15. Then He will preserve those whom He can forgive,
 And at the same time destroy those who are
 polluted with sins.]

LXXXVI. When, therefore, ye receive this my epistle, read it in your congregations with care. 2. And meditate thereon, above all on the days of your fasts. 3. And bear me in mind by means of this epistle, as I also bear you in mind in it, and always fare ye well."

LXXXVII. **The Epistle to the nine and a half Tribes is sent.**

LXXXVII. And it came to pass when I had ended all the words of this epistle, and had written it sedulously to its close, that I folded it, and sealed it carefully, and bound it to the neck of the eagle, and dismissed and sent it.

HERE ENDETH THE BOOK OF BARUCH, THE SON OF NERIAH.

PRINTED IN GREAT BRITAIN BY RICHARD CLAY & SONS, LIMITED,
BRUNSWICK ST., STAMFORD ST., S.E. I, AND BUNGAY, SUFFOLK.

The Assumption of Moses
Translated by William John Ferrar

THE ASSUMPTION OF MOSES

I. 1–18. **Moses, about to die, appoints Joshua as his successor, delivering to him the books to bury safely.**

I. 1. [The book of the prophecy of Moses, which was made in the one hundred and twentieth year of his life,][1] 2. That is two thousand five hundred years from the Creation of the world; 3. Or, according to Eastern reckoning, two thousand seven hundred years,[2] and four hundred [3] from the exodus from Phœnicia, 4. When the people had gone forth after the exodus that was made by Moses to Amman [4] beyond the Jordan,[5]

[1] The opening words are lost. Above is Clemen's restoration. Charles from analogy of Test. xii. Patr. reads : " Testamentum Moysi, quæ præcepit año vitæ ejus Cmo et XXmo."

[2] As emended by Charles and Clemen.

[3] Exod. xii. 40 (Mass. text), gives 430 years. Gen. xv. 13 can mean either 400 or 430; cf. Acts vii. 6.

[4] Amman—in the tribe of Gad.

[5] Note Gentile adaptations in the passage. Moses could not have spoken thus.

5. The prophecy [1] that was made by Moses in the book Deuteronomy, 6. When he called unto him Joshua the son of Nun, a man approved of the Lord, 7. Who should be the minister of the people [2] and of the tabernacle of the testimony with all its holy things; 8. And should bring the people into the land that was given to their fathers, [3] 9. That it should be given to them by the covenant and the oath which He spake in the tabernacle to give it by Joshua, [4] and he spake to Joshua these words: 10. Promise [5] to perform with all diligence whatsoever thou hast been commanded, that thou mayest so act as to be blameless before God. [6] 11. These things said the Lord of the world. For He created the world on account of His own people, 13. Though He began not to make

---

[1] " profetiæ " = " profetia," as often in late Latin.

[2] " successor   plebi " :   evidently   equivalent   of διάδοχος, chief minister of the king in LXX (1 Chron. xviii. 17; 2 Chron. xxvi. 11). Used of Joshua (Josh. i. 1). See Num. xi. 28 and viii. 26.

[3] " patribus," emended by Charles from " ex tribus."

[4] See Deut. xxxi. 14, 20 and 23. Text " de Josum," for agent.

[5] " Et promitte." Charles emends " ⟨Be strong⟩ and of a good courage."

[6] Charles emends " sis deo " for " est ideo." Clemen puts stop at " est," and reads " is blameless. Thereforth thus saith . . ."

manifest this purpose [1] of creation from the beginning of the world, that the Gentiles might be confounded on the matter, and to their shame might confound one another in arguments. 14. And so He planned and ordained me, who before of old was prepared to be the mediator of His covenant.[2] 15. And now I tell you that the time of the years of my life is finished and I pass to sleep with my fathers in the sight of all the people.[3] . . . 16. And read thou [4] this writing that thou mayest have regard to the safe-keeping of the books,[5] 17. Which I shall deliver thee, which thou shalt arrange and smear with oil of cedar, and lay up in vessels of earthenware in the place which God made from the beginning of the creation of the world, 18. That His Name might be called on (there) even to

[1] "inceptionem." As to the idea Charles says, "the prevalent Jewish view from the first century onwards; cf. 4 Ezra vi. 55, 59; vii. 11; 2 Baruch xiv. 18."

[2] Quoted by Gelasius of Cyzicum (Comm. Act. Syn Nic. ii. 18). Note that Moses is regarded as pre-existent. The title "mediator" is not given to him in the Old Testament. It is implied in Heb. viii. 6; ix. 5; xii. 24, and is common in writings of the first century A.D.

[3] There is no suggestion of an Assumption here.

[4] Charles supplies " tu."

[5] i.e. The Pentateuch.

the day of repentance in the visitation,[1] wherewith the Lord will visit them in the consummation
of the end of the days.

II. 1-9. Prophecy of the taking of Canaan, the Judges, and the Kings, to the revolt of the ten tribes, and the beginning of idolatry.

II. 1. . . .[2] they shall go by thee into the land,
which He decreed and promised to give to their
fathers, 2. In which thou shalt bless them, and
shalt give and establish to each one his portion
in me,[3] and shalt establish for them a kingdom,
and shalt set[4] lawgivers over their districts,[5]
according to that which shall please the Lord
in righteousness and judgement. 3. . . .[6] And,
when they shall have entered into the land [five]
years, afterwards chiefs and kings shall have the

[1] Cf. Luke i. 79; xix. 44 (the coming of the Kingdom).

[2] Charles supplies " et nunc."

[3] Cf. 2 Sam. xx. 1.

[4] " dimittes."

[5] " magisteria locorum." Charles translates " pre-
fectures " and compares Deut. xvi. 18; 1 Chron. xxiii.
4.

[6] Charles supplies " And it shall come to pass " and
" five."

dominion for eighteen years,[1] and for nineteen years the ten tribes shall break off from them,[2] 4. For the two [3] tribes shall depart, and transfer the tabernacle of the testimony.[4] Then the God of heaven shall build the wall [5] of His tabernacle, and the tower [6] of His sanctuary, and the two tribes of His holiness shall be placed there; 5. For the ten tribes shall establish their kingdom according to their devices; 6. And they shall bring their victims to the altar for twenty [7] years; 7. And seven [8] shall entrench the walls, and I will protect nine, and four shall transgress the [9]

[1] A year stands for a period of rule. Thus the fifteen judges, and Saul, David and Solomon are the " eighteen years." And the kings from Rehoboam to Hoshea the " nineteen years."

[2] Text is " abrumpent tib." Charles emends " se abrumpent tribus."

[3] Charles emends to " twelve."

[4] Text " testimony of the tabernacle."

[5] Text has " palam." Charles emends to " aulam." Clemen " palum."

[6] Text " ferrum." Charles emends to " turrem " : quoting 1 Enoch lxxxix. 50, 67, 73.

[7] i. e. the twenty kings of Judah including Athaliah.

[8] The " seven " are Rehoboam, Abijah, Asa, Jehoshaphat, Jehoram, Ahaziah, Athaliah.

The " nine " are Joash, Amaziah, Uzziah, Jotham, Ahaz, Hezekiah, Manasseh, Amon, Josiah; and the " four " Jehoahaz, Jehoiakim, Jehoiachin, and Zedekiah.

[9] Text " adcedent ad," i. e. προσβήσονται, which the Greek translator mistook for παραβήσονται (Charles).

covenant of the Lord, and profane the oath,[1] which the Lord made with them.   8. And they shall sacrifice their children to strange gods, and shall set up idols in the tabernacle [2] to serve them.   9. And they shall work abomination in the house of the Lord, and grave every kind [3] of beast even many idols.

III. 1–14. The Captivity under Nebuchadnezzar, and the united prayer of the divided tribes in their Captivity.

III. 1. . . .[4] in those times shall come on them a king from the East,[5] and his horsemen shall cover their land,   2. And shall burn their " colony " [6] with fire with the holy temple of the Lord, and he shall take away all the holy vessels;[7] 3. And he shall drive out all the people, and lead them into his own land, even the two tribes shall

[1] Text is " finem," *i. e.* Greek ὅρον corrupt for ὅρκον (Charles).

[2] " idola scenæ," for " scenā." Clemen emends " idola obscena," with Rönsch.

[3] Text " omnem animalium." Charles supplies " similitudinem."

[4] Supply " et."   [5] Nebuchadnezzar, 586 B.C.

[6] If this word is to be taken literally, the Latin translation must have been made after A.D. 135, when Hadrian made Jerusalem a Roman " colony."

[7] 2 Chron. xxxvi. 7.

he lead with him.   4. Then the two tribes shall
call on the ten tribes and shall be led[1] like a
lioness on the dusty plains hungering and thirst-
ing with their little children,   5. And they shall
cry : " Righteous and holy is the Lord, inasmuch
as ye have sinned, and we likewise are led into
captivity with you."   6. Then the ten tribes
shall wail when they hear the reproachful words
of the two tribes,   7. And shall say : " What
have we done unto you, brethren ?   Hath not
this tribulation fallen on the whole house of
Israel ? "   8. And all the tribes shall wail, crying
to heaven and saying :   9. " God of Abraham, God
of Isaac, God of Jacob, remember Thy covenant which Thou madest with them, and the oath,
which Thou swarest unto them by Thyself, that
their seed should never fail from the land, which
Thou gavest them."   10. Then shall they remember me on that day saying one tribe to another
and each man to his neighbour :   11. " Lo ! is
not this that which Moses did once declare unto
us in prophecies, who suffered many things in
Egypt, and in the Red Sea, and in the desert
forty years ?[2]   12. Yea, he declared and called

---

[1] Text is " ducent se."   Charles suggests a corruption
of ἀχθέσονται (will be angry) into ἀχθήσονται.

[2] Acts vii. 36.

heaven and earth to witness against us, that we
should not transgress the commandments of the
Lord, of which he was the mediator to us.   13.
And these things[1] have come upon us from him
according to his words, and according to his
assurance, as he bore witness to us in those times,
yea, they have been fulfilled even to our being
led captive into the East?"   14. And   these
shall be in captivity about seventy-seven years.[2]

IV. 1-9. **The Prayer of Daniel, and the Return of the two tribes.**

IV. 1. Then one[3] shall enter, that shall be over
them, and he shall spread forth his hands, and
kneel upon his knees and pray for them saying :
2. " Lord of all, King on Thy lofty seat, That
rulest over the world, That didst will that this
people should be unto Thee a peculiar people,
and Thou didst will to be called their God according to the Covenant, which Thou madest with
their fathers.   3. And they went as captives

[1] " Quæ " corrupt for " ecce ea " (Charles).
[2] Charles suggests that this means " an indefinite
period," cf. Matt. xviii. 22.   It modifies Jer. xxv. 11,
which is interpreted by Daniel ix. 24 as seventy weeks of
years, i. e. 490.
[3] Daniel.

to a strange land with their wives and children, and around[1] the gates of strangers, and where there is great vanity;[2] 4. Have respect unto them and pity them, O Lord of heaven." 5. Then God will remember them because of the covenant, which He made with their fathers and will show forth His mercy also in those times. 6. And He will put it into the mind of a king[3] to have pity on them, and he shall send them back to their own land and country. 7. Then shall some part of the tribes go up and come to the place appointed for them and shall entrench the place anew. 8. And the two tribes shall remain in the faith laid down for them, sad and groaning, because they cannot offer sacrifice to the Lord God of their fathers.[4] 9. And the ten tribes shall increase and spread among[5] the Gentiles in the time of their tribulation.

[1] Text " circa."

[2] Text " majestas," Clemen and Charles ματαιότης; through μεγαλειότης (Charles).

[3] Cyrus, Ezra i. 1-4.

[4] Charles notes the low value set on the worship of the restored temple; cf. 2 Bar. lxviii. 5, 6; Hag. ii. 3; Ezra iii. 12; Mal. i. 7.

[5] Text " devenient apud natos in tempore tribuum (tribum)." Charles supposes a corruption of the Hebrew text, and makes "devenient" = "multiplicabuntur." "Natos" is for "nationes." He translates "devenient"

V. 1-6. **Idolatry of the Priests under Antiochus and the Hellenizers.**

V. 1. And when the day of reckoning shall draw nigh, and vengeance shall arise at the hand of the kings [1] who are partakers of their evil deeds, and punishers of them,   2. They themselves also shall be divided as to the truth,   3. According as it hath been said : [2] " They shall turn aside from righteousness, and approach to iniquity, and shall defile with pollutions [3] the house of their captivity, and shall lust after strange gods." 4. For they shall forsake the truth of God ; but there shall be those who shall pollute the altar . . . even with their gifts, [4] which they offer to the Lord, not being priests, but slaves born of slaves.   5. And those who are their lawgivers, [5] their teachers,

---

by " will be multiplied," and "tribum" by "captivity," "increase and multiply among the nations in the time of their captivity."

[1] " de reges."

[2] " fatum fuit," for " factum fuit."

[3] " ingenationibus."

[4] Charles supplies " ipsis." He refers this to the Hellenizing High-priests Jason and Menelaus, who preceded the Maccabees ; the latter was a Benjamite. Cf. 2 Macc. iv. 13, 19, 20 ; v. 8, and iii. 4 ; iv. 23.

[5] " Qui enim magistri sunt," emended by Charles to " the many " or " the Rabbis."

in those days shall have respect unto men's persons for reward and receive gifts and pervert justice by receiving bribes.[1] 6. And it shall come to pass that the whole colony and the bounds of their habitations shall be filled with sins and iniquities . . . their judges [2] shall be those who work unrighteousness against the Lord, and they shall give judgement for money according as each man desireth.[3]

VI. 1–9. The evil Hasmonæans, and the reign of Herod—Conquest by Varus [B.C. 4].

VI. 1. Then shall arise over them kings [4] to reign and they shall be called priests of the Most

---

[1] " Erunt mirantes personas cupiditatum et acceptiones munerum et pervendent justitias accipiendo poenas." Charles emends " accipientes," translates " personas cupiditatum " " desirable persons," puts " pervertent " for " pervendent," and brackets " accipiendo poenas " as a gloss.

[2] The " dittography " in the text is obvious. " A deo ut qui facit erunt impii judices " and " a domino qui faciunt erunt impii judices," " the first and inferior version was intended to be deleted " (Charles).

[3] " inerunt in campo judicare." Charles supposes ἐν ἀγρῷ a mistake for ἐν ἀργύρῳ.

[4] The Maccabees. Jonathan High-priest, 153 B.C. Office hereditary, 141 B.C.

High God, and they shall verily work impiety in the Holy of Holies. 2. And to them shall succeed a self-willed king,[1] who shall not be of the priestly line, a rash and wicked man, and he shall judge them as they deserve. 3. He shall cut off their chief men with the sword and bury[2] them in unknown places, so that no man may know where their bodies rest. 4. He shall slay old men and young men and shall not spare. 5. Then shall there be bitter fear of him among them in their land, 6. And he shall execute judgement upon them, as did the Egyptians, for thirty and four years, and shall punish them. . . . 7. And he shall beget sons that shall succeed him and reign for shorter periods.[3] 8. Into their parts[4] shall come the strong[5] and a mighty Western[6]

[1] " rex petulans," *i. e.* Herod the Great.

[2] Text " singuli." Clemen emends to " sepeliet." Charles " stinguet."

[3] Text " . . . et . . . roducit natos . . . eccedentes sibi breviora tempora donarent." Charles " et producet natos qui succedentes sibi breviora tempora dominarent." So Clemen. Herod reigned 34 years, Antipas 43, Philip 37. See Introduction, p. 9.

[4] Text " pares."

[5] Text " mortis," emended " fortes " (Clemen), " cohortes " (Charles).

[6] " occidentes." P. Quinctilius Varus, Governor of Syria, quelled a rebellion in 4 B.C. (Jos. Ant. xvii. 10, 1 *sqq.*).

king, who shall conquer them,   9. And lead them captive and burn part of their temple with fire, and crucify some around their " colony."

VII. 1–10. **The Rulers of the Writer's own time.**

.VII. 1. And after this the times shall be finished, in a moment shall follow the second course[1] . . . the four hours shall come.   2. They shall be forced[2]. . . .   3. And in their day shall reign pestilent and impious men claiming to be righteous.[3]   4. And these shall excite the wrath of their own friends,[4] who will be cunning men, deceitful in all their own affairs, and at every hour of the day bent on feasting,   5. Gluttons, gourmands . . .   6. Devourers of poor men's[5] goods and saying that they do these things for mercy's[6] sake . . .   7. So that they may de-

[1] Text " momento . . . etur cursus a . . ." Merx " sequetur." Charles " finietur," " alter " for " a."

[2] This verse " defies translation " (Charles).

[3] Charles refers this attack to the Sadducees, comparing Pss. of Solomon.

[4] Text " animorum " emended by Clemen to " amicorum." Charles retains " animorum," but makes " viam " a mistranslation of the Hebrew (Greek ἰόν, poison).

[5] " (paup-)erum." A hopeless lacuna precedes.

[6] " misericordiam ; " Charles " justice."

stroy them, querulous,[1] false, hiding themselves
so as not to be known, impious in sin, and full
of iniquity from sunrise to sunset, saying : 8.
" Give us banquets and luxury, let us eat and
drink : and we will reckon ourselves great men."
9. And their hands and minds shall traffic with
the unclean, and their mouth speak great things,[2]
and moreover they shall say : 10. " Touch me
not, lest thou shouldst pollute me where I
stand." [3] . . . .

VIII. 1–5. "The King of the Kings of the Earth " will persecute the faithful.

VIII. 1.[4] And so great . . . vengeance and
wrath shall come on them, such [5] as hath not been

---

[1] Text " quæru-. . . ."

[2] " ingentia." Cf. Dan. vii. 8, 20; Jude 16.

[3] Again the text is quite hopeless.

[4] Charles considers this " second visitation " can
only refer to the persecution of Antiochus Epiphanes,
and boldly transfers chaps. viii. and ix. to the gap between
chaps. v. and vi., where such an account is not out of
place. Burkitt (Hastings, *D.B.*, art. "Assumption of
Moses ") does not accept this. " The final Theophany (x.)
comes in very well after the story of the ideal saint,
Taxo (ix.), and very badly after the description of the
wicked priests and rulers of chap. vii." He refers it to
the stories of the Antiochian martyrs.

[5] Cf. Matt. xxiv. 21.

in the land from the beginning even to that time, in which God shall raise against them the king of the kings of the earth and a potentate of mighty power,[1] who will crucify those who acknowledge their circumcision, 2. And torture those who deny[2] it, and deliver them to be led bound to prison, and their wives will be divided among the gentiles.[3] 3. And their sons will be treated by surgeons so as to make circumcision of none effect.[4] 4. And some of them shall be punished by torments and fire and sword, and shall be forced to carry[5] their idols publicly, as defiled as those who possess them. 5. And by their tormentors they shall be forced to enter into the hidden place, and they shall be forced with goads to blaspheme the sacred word[6] insolently, yea, and last of all the laws, and what they have upon their altar.[7]

[1] The Antichrist. Charles "Antiochus IV."

[2] " negantes " for " necantes."   " Charles " celantes."

[3] Text " diisdonabuntur."   Clemen " disdon.," *i. e.* distributed.   Charles " shall be given to the gods among the Gentiles," quoting 2 Macc. vi. 4, for Cult of Venus.

[4] Cf. Jos. Ant. XII. v. 1; 1 Macc. i. 15; 1 Cor. vii. 18.

[5] " bajulare," cf. 2 Macc. vi. 7.

[6] " Verbum " = λόγος—in late Hebrew. " The person of God " (Charles).

[7] " quod haberent supra altarium suum "—with Charles " the sacrifice "; cf. Matt. xxiii. 18.

C

IX. 1-7. Taxo (the Ideal Patriot) will protest by dying of starvation with his sons in the wilderness.

IX. 1. Then while this man ruleth a man of the tribe of Levi whose name will be TAXO,[1] who having seven sons shall speak to them and ask them : 2. " See ye, my sons, how a second cruel and shameless vengeance hath fallen on the people, and a punishment without mercy beyond the measure of the first ? [2] 3. For what nation or what country or what people of those who disobey the Lord, who have wrought much sin, have suffered as much as hath been our portion ? 4. Now therefore, my sons, listen to me : for ye see and know, that neither your parents nor their forefathers ever tempted [3] God, in transgressing His commands. 5. And ye know how that this is our strength. Now let us do this : 6. Let us fast three days, and on the fourth day let us enter the cave, which is in the

[1] The name TAXO transliterated into Hebrew as TAXOC by the use of a common cipher becomes Eleazar (2 Macc. vi. 18 *sq.* and 4 Macc. v. 3). With his story is here amalgamated that of the widow's seven sons (2 Macc. vii.) ; and his " cave " corresponds to that of the Chasids (1 Macc. i. 53 ; ii. 31).

[2] Text " eminent principatum " read " eminens."

[3] " temptans," corrupt for " temptantes."

field, and there let us die, rather than transgress the commandments of the Lord of Lords, the God of our fathers. 7. For if we do this and die, our blood shall be avenged in the sight of the Lord.

X. 1–15. The coming of God's Kingdom, and the Vindication of the Righteous by God Himself.

X. 1. And then His kingdom shall appear through His whole creation.
And then the devil [1] shall have an end,
And sadness shall be taken away with him.

2. Then the hands of the Angel [2] shall be filled,
Who is established in the highest,
Who shall straightway avenge them of their adversaries.

3. . . . For the Heavenly One shall arise from the throne of His kingdom,
And shall come out of His holy habitation
With indignation and wrath for His children.

4. And the earth shall quake : even to its bounds shall it be shaken :
And the lofty mountains shall be brought low and shall be shaken,

---

[1] Zabulus.   [2] Michael as in Dan. xii. 1.

And the valleys shall fall.[1]

5. The sun shall not give his light, and the horns of the moon shall be turned into darkness,

   And they shall be broken, and the whole of the moon shall be turned into blood.[2]

   And the circuit[3] of the stars shall be disordered;

6. And the sea shall fall even to the abyss;

   The fountains of waters shall fail,

   And the rivers be afraid.[4]

7. Because the Most High God, the Eternal, the Only God shall arise,

   And manifest Himself to punish the nations,

   And to destroy all their idols.

8. Then shalt thou be happy, thou O Israel,

   And shalt mount on the neck and wings of the eagle,

---

[1] " et concutientur et convalles cadent." Charles reads " et colles concutientur," comparing Isa. xl. 4.

[2] Charles, altering the text translates, " And the horns of the sun shall be broken, and he shall be turned into darkness; and the moon shall not give her light, and be turned wholly into blood." Cf. Joel ii. 10; iii. 15; Isa. xiii. 10; Matt. xxiv. 29; Mark xiii. 24; Luke xxiii. 45; Acts ii. 20; Rev. vi. 12; ix. 2.

[3] " orbis."

[4] " expavescent." Charles " exarescent " = " shall dry up."

And (the Days of thy sorrow) shall be ended.[1]

9. And God shall exalt thee,
   And bring thee to the heaven of the stars,
   The place of His habitation.

10. And thou shalt look [2] from on high, and be-
    hold thy adversaries on the earth,[3]
    And shalt know them and rejoice,
    And give thanks, and acknowledge thy
    Creator.

11. "Now must thou, Joshua son of Nun,
keep these words and this book; 12. For there
shall be from my death and assumption [4] even to
His Coming two hundred and fifty times,[5] which
shall pass. 13. And this is the course of the
times [6] . . . which they shall finish, until they
are consummated. 14. But I go to sleep with my
fathers : 15. Wherefore be thou, Joshua, son

---

[1] Supplying " dies luctus tui " (Cheyne). Charles
suggests, altering text :

   " Thou shalt go up against the eagle,
     And its necks and wings shall be destroyed."

[2] " conspicies " for " conspiges."

[3] Text " in terram " = $\gamma\hat{\eta}$. Charles very reasonably
suggests " the valley," *i. e.* Gehenna; cf. Isa. lxvi. 24;
1 Enoch xxvii. 2, 3.

[4] " receptione " : Charles makes this a gloss by
the editor.

[5] *i. e.* 250 year-weeks = 1,750 years.

[6] Text " . . . horum."

of Nun, strong; God hath chosen thee in my
place to be the minister of the same covenant."

XI. 1-19. **Humility of Joshua ; how can he lead so many Israelites ?**

XI. 1. And when Joshua had heard the words
of Moses, which were thus written in his writing,
even all that he before had said, he rent his clothes
and fell at his feet.[1]   2. And Moses exhorted him,
and wept with him.   3. And Joshua answered
him and said :   4. " Why comfortest [2] thou me,
Lord Moses, and how shall I be comforted, for
that bitter word thou spakest, which hath gone
forth from thy mouth, which is full of tears and
groans, in that thou dost depart from this people
· . .   5. What place shall receive thee . . .   6.
Or what shall be the monument of thy sepulchre,
7. Or who shall dare to bear thy body as that of a
man from one place to another?   8. For to all
who die there are sepulchres on the earth according to their age; but thy sepulchre shall be from
the rising sun to the setting and from the south
to the bounds of the north, the whole earth shall
be thy sepulchre.[3]   9. O My Lord, thou passest

---

[1] Text " pedes meos ; " Charles " pedes Moysi."
[2] " solares " and " solabor " for " celares " and
" celabor."   [3] Cf. Thuc. ii.

hence, and who shall feed this people, 10. Or who is there to have pity on them, who to lead them in the way, 11. Or to pray for them, not forbearing [1] even for a single day, that I may bring them into the land of their forefathers? 12. How shall I govern this people, even as a father his only son or a lady her virgin-daughter,[2] prepared to be given [3] to a husband, who feareth lest the sun light on her body, and lest she should run on the ground with unshod feet? . . . 13. How shall I provide them with food and drink according to the pleasure of their will? [4] . . . 14. For of them there are 100,000 [5] men, since to so great a number have they increased through thy prayers, my Lord Moses. 15. And what wisdom or understanding have I to give judgement or to give answers by speech in the house (of the Lord)? 16. Yea, and the kings of the Amorites, when they hear that we are attacking them, thinking that there is no longer among them a

[1] Text "nec patiens" = οὐδέ παριείς—"not omitting" (Charles).

[2] Text "tamquam filiam dominam virginem." Either "dominam" = κυρίαν meaning "his own," or change to "domina," as above translated.

[3] "dari" for "tali" (Charles).

[4] So Charles, changing "voluntatem voluntatis" to "voluptatem voluntatis."

[5] Charles inserts D (600,000) from Exod. xii. 37.

holy spirit manifold and incomprehensible, worthy of the Lord, the master of the Word, faithful in all things, the divine prophet [1] of the earth, and the world's perfect teacher—no longer among them, will say : ' Let us go against them.   17. If their enemies should once now do impious deeds against their Lord, they have no champion now to bear prayers on their behalf to the Lord, as was Moses the great messenger, who every hour by day and night had his knees fixed to the ground praying and beholding Him Who is omnipotent over the world [2] in mercy and justice, reminding Him of the covenant of the fathers and by his oath propitiating the Lord.'   18. For they will say : ' He is no more with them ; let us go and confound them from off the face of the earth.'   19. What then shall happen to thy people, my Lord Moses ? "

XII. 1–13. Moses encourages Joshua, and sets him in his own seat.

XII. 1. And when Joshua had finished these words, he fell again at the feet of Moses.   2. And

[1] Text " divinum . . . profetem." Charles " God's chief prophet."

[2] Text " et intuens homini potentem orbem." Charles reads, " potentem omnis orbis." Hilgenfeld suggests as above " omnipotentem orbem."

Moses took his hand, and raised him into the seat
before him.   And he answered and said to him :
3. " Joshua, despise not thyself,[1] but show thyself
unmoved, and attend to my words.   4. God
created all the nations, which are on the face of
the earth, and us as well; He foresaw them and
us from the beginning of the creation of the earth
even to the end of the world, and nothing is
by Him neglected, however small it be, but He
foresaw all things and foreknew[2] . . .   5. All
things which should be in this world, He foresaw
and lo ! it is brought forth. . . .   6. And me
He formed to pray for them and for their sins
. . . and to intercede for them.   7. For not
because of any virtue or strength[3] of mine, but
of His good pleasure[4] his mercy and patience have
been mine.   8. Yea I tell thee, Joshua; not
because of the piety of this people wilt thou
destroy the nations.   9. All that is in heaven and
the foundations of the earth were made and
approved[5] by God, and are beneath the signet[6]

[1] " te " for " et."

[2] Text is here very corrupt.   Charles reads " pro-
movit cuncta " = " caused all to come forth."

[3] Text is " infirmitatem."

[4] Text " temperantius " = $\epsilon\pi\iota\epsilon\iota\kappa\epsilon\sigma\tau\epsilon\rho\sigma\nu$, representing
the Hebrew of above.   [5] Text " ut provata."

[6] Text " nullo " emended to " annulo."

of His right hand.   10. They that perform and carry out the commandments of God flourish and tread a good path;   11. But sinners and they who neglect His commandments lack the good things,[1] which are foretold.   And they shall be punished by the nations with many torments; 12. Yet it is not possible that He should wholly destroy and forsake[2] them.   13. For God hath gone forth, Who foresaw all things from the beginning, and His covenant is established even by the oath, which . . ."

[1] Text " carere bonam."
[2] " relinquet."   Charles emends to " extinguat."

PRINTED IN GREAT BRITAIN BY RICHARD CLAY & SONS, LIMITED, BRUNSWICK ST., STAMFORD ST., S.E. 1, AND BUNGAY, SUFFOLK.

To Our Readers

Weiser Books, an imprint of Red Wheel/Weiser, publishes books across the entire spectrum of occult and esoteric subjects. Our mission is to publish quality books that will make a difference in people's lives without advocating any one particular path or field of study. We value the integrity, originality, and depth of knowledge of our authors.

Our readers are our most important resource, and we value your input, suggestions, and ideas about what you would like to see published. Please feel free to contact us, to request our latest book catalog, or to be added to our mailing list.

Red Wheel/Weiser, LLC
P.O. Box 612
York Beach, ME 03910-0612
www.redwheelweiser.com